MOTOWN:
THE VIEW FROM THE BOTTOM

MOTOWN:
THE VIEW FROM THE
BOTTOM

JACK ASHFORD
with CHARLENE ASHFORD

MOTOWN: THE VIEW FROM THE BOTTOM

First published 2003

ISBN 1-904408-20-6

Published by BANK HOUSE BOOKS

Designed and typeset in England by
BANK HOUSE BOOKS
PO Box 3
NEW ROMNEY
TN29 9WJ

Front cover photograph by Karen Sas
© Elliot Scott Productions LLC

CONTENTS

FOREWORD BY MARTHA REEVES

I'm excited for the musicians. Not only is there a movie interest in their part of the Motown sound, here comes their memoirs. I have been one of their biggest cheerleaders. I let everyone who allows me the privilege to be interviewed know that these great jazz cats gave us a chance to be heard by playing the finest sounds from heaven, and leaving some space for vocals.

Jack Ashford not only inspired me to pick up a tambourine and hold my tempos as I attempted to fit the words into the bars of music hand written for us at Hitsville USA, the Funk Brothers that Jack was a permanent part of never played too fast, or too loud for the star of the moment.

He also plays a sweet rhythm on the vibes. There are plenty of Motown hits to attest to that.

He was always on time, and right out when he was done. I tell everyone that there were never any confrontations in our presence, and the men and women working out our hits that have lasted through four decades all knew us, and gave us the love and inspiration we needed to sing, dance, and bring the songs to life.

We gave Berry Gordy his dream come true, and filled the world with the 'sound of young America'.

On our first Motown Revue, Jack taught us about discipline, and how to make a meal of popcorn and sardines, by following it with a lot of water. That got some of us through the night.

Thanks to the Funk Brothers, we were all enabled to perfect our own sounds, and personal styles. We were all featured and unique. Our music sounded better than the recorded versions when we performed together for the Dusty Springfield special in 1964, with Smokey Robinson and the Miracles, Marvin Gaye, Stevie Wonder, The Supremes, The Temptations, and Martha Reeves and the Vandellas – my first experience working with them outside of the studio.

Jack was always a tall, dark and handsome cool cat.

His student.
Love and God bless
MARTHA REEVES

Author's Note

I am grateful to Motown's owner, Berry Gordy, for the opportunity of being a small part in its phenomenal history. Those years were the most memorable years of my life. Whilst wading through the maze of past experiences surrounding me at Motown, I found that, after forty years, some of my recollections were as clear as crystal. I would like to thank the Funk Brothers for their support and help in reconstructing some of our vanished yesterdays. Any failure to mention certain people or events by myself or my co-author is simply an oversight. My sincere thanks to anyone that played a role in helping with the publication of this book.

JACK ASHFORD

> *This book is dedicated to:*
> *my mother, THELMA ASHFORD,*
> *my father, ROLAND ASHFORD,*
> *my brother, ALBERT GROSE*
> *and my wife, CHARLENE ASHFORD*

MY EARLY YEARS

The day I was born, my mom said it was the happiest day of her life. "Our hearts danced from one end of the block to the other." My parents had wished for a girl, because I had an older brother (Al), and five uncles. I was rather long in length at birth (24 inches). Everybody proclaimed that I would be a tall guy because of my family genes. My mother, Thelma was about five foot eight, and my father Roland was six foot two. A couple of my uncles were more than six feet tall in my father's family. So with me growing to giant size six foot five was no real surprise. I take top honors as the tallest person in my family.

My mother was a domestic worker and my father was a laborer. He was in and out of our lives. Eventually the final chapter of my parents' relationship was written and closed. He was gone for good. I never knew what happened because my mom never said anything about their break up. I could only imagine that it was another woman, since they divorced and dad remarried. Since 'Papa was a rolling stone', I was reared by my mom, her two sisters and her five brothers. The house was very crowded with ten people to share a three-bedroom home in Arlington Street in North Philadelphia. I saw very little of my dad, and grew up thinking I would never see him again. But with five uncles living with me, they kept me well trained and gave me plenty of advice. In spite of all the masculine association with my uncles, I still thought of my dad. I remembered how he loved classical music and orange sherbet ice cream. I couldn't mention his name, but in my heart I missed him. He never tried to contact me and many years passed before I tried to contact him. In fact, I was thirty-eight years old when I saw him again.

More than thirty years had passed. I had gotten dad's address from my Uncle Base, and decided to look him up. I was somewhat anxious about seeing him. I feared the worst – that he would turn me away. After the elapse of so many years, we really didn't know each other and I tried to imagine what our conversation would be like.

The walkway to the house was only a few steps, but it seemed like it took forever to reach the door. I rang the doorbell and no one answered. My wife was with me and insisted that I try again. No one responded.

Just as we were about to walk away, the inside door opened slowly. He barely cracked the door and spoke through the glass storm-door: "Yes, may I help you sir? Who are you looking for?"

I stood speechless, staring at how thirty years had altered my father's appearance. His sight seemed to have been failing and his body was frail and aged. "D-D-Dad it's me. It's your son," I responded nervously.

"Is that you J-Jack?" He was as nervous as I was. He just couldn't believe that it was really me. "Well, come on in, son. This is really a big surprise. He reached for me and we just clung to each other for a long time. It wasn't enough to make up for lost years, but I could feel the silent message his heart was transmitting. His voice had a brittle tone and he asked "How have you been?" I wanted to tell him how much I had missed him or ask why he left us. Somehow I just couldn't. Instead, I gave him the usual "I've been doing fine" answer. I introduced him to my wife, Char, and granddaughter, Miko. He was happy to know that he had a daughter-in-law and a granddaughter. My youngest daughter Jakene hadn't been born yet.

Our awkwardness was evident throughout the visit. At times, the room would become filled with silence or parts of our conversation would be repeated. When it was time to go, Dad repeated again how glad and surprised he was to see me. He said he was very sick and would appreciate another visit from me. That was the last time I saw my dad alive. I was glad that my wife had encouraged me to visit him. Less than a year after that, I received a telegram that Dad had passed away.

There were musicians in my mom's family as well as my dad's family. Uncle Gordon 'Base' Ashford was a left hand upright bass player who played only jazz. He was well respected by some of the big name musicians like Coltrane and others of that genre. My uncle could really play, and was a great role model who encouraged me to play music and stay out of trouble. He lived in North Philadelphia on 21st Street, near Berks. This corner was a popular teen hangout. During those days, guys would congregate on the corners and croon with flawless harmony. That's where some of the locals got their start. My other uncle, Jerome Ashford, played saxophone. Man, he could really 'jam'. He once said: "When I die, I want to be on the bandstand playing," and that's exactly how he died. He suffered a massive heart attack while performing. Uncle 'Base' would introduce me to some of the jazz players that he played with from time to time. I was impressed seeing Philly Joe Jones, Ray Bryant, Sonny Stitt, Redds Garland, John Coltrane and others. It was like meeting the 'High Gods of Jazz'. This was every young man's dream. All of my friends were jazz enthusiasts and knew very little about any other music, other than what we heard in church on Sunday.

MY EARLY YEARS

I attended the same music school as John Coltrane and Kenny Dennis. The Granoff School of Music was located on Walnut Street in Philadelphia. At times it was hard for me to totally focus because I was in the same room as two of my idols. We all took theory classes, and finished together. That was a real experience. Kenny Dennis married Nancy Wilson, and later became a very impressive executive with the Musicians' Union. Kenny was a drummer with John Coltrane.

My mother's mother played piano. We would all gather around the piano to enjoy her eloquent style of playing and singing. I can remember when I was about six years old, my favorite spot was to stand right beside her and watch her fingers effortlessly glide over the ebony and ivory keys. She would complete a repertoire of songs, and never failed to play my favorite song, 'There'll Be Blue Birds Over The White Cliffs of Dover'. I really loved that song. I would sometimes seat myself at the piano and attempt to emulate my grandmother when no one was around. I was greatly impressed with my grandmother Lena's playing, but it wasn't the first time I had expressed an interest in music. When I was about four years old, my mother gave me a drum for Christmas. She would place me on top of the dining room table with my drums and I would play along with the Victrola. The table represented the stage and my aunts and uncles were the audience. They would applaud my playing, and I would bow in appreciation of their indulgence. They enjoyed it and marveled at my almost perfect timing. "Bravo, Bravo, Jackie!" My mom would always encourage me and say "One day you'll be a real star on a real stage."

"I believe you might have yourself a drummer," or "I bet Jackie will some day be a real good musician" my uncles declared. In my mind I thought then that I was a real star on a real stage. It seemed so natural to me. I'm sure those invaluable moments inspired me to pursue music beyond the realms of family entertainment.

Sometimes in life there are experiences that make indelible impressions, and vivid pictures seem to become etched in your heart and mind forever. When I was eleven years old something happened that I shall never forget that seemed to have guided the course of my life.

It happened on a very cold wintry night. The ground was frozen over with several inches of snow. Icicles two or three feet long hung down like diamond cones from the house roofs. The moon was full and bright. The light from the moon was just enough to illuminate the snow and it seemed almost like day. The wind was still; blue crisp temperature dictated a need for a heavy coat, gloves, and a wool scarf around the neck. I was living in Arlington Street, and on this very cold night my aunt Connie wanted me to go to the corner store for a pack of Phillip Morris cigarettes.

This was great for me because I loved the snow. I immediately got my wraps on and was off to the store in no time. Aside from loving the snow, I also loved the pinball machine that was at the store. When I arrived there, I saw my friend Earl playing it. I stood there for a few minutes watching him, and when he left I played a game or two. After finishing the game, I asked the storekeeper for the Phillip Morris cigarettes, but he was out of that brand. I headed for home to find out if my aunt wanted a substitute. Upon entering the house everyone was very hostile toward me. I couldn't figure it out.

I asked my aunt, "Why is everybody mad at me?"

She shouted "Earl and his mother just left here!"

Did I hear right? I asked myself and repeated out loud, "Earl and his mother just left here?"

My uncle quickly answered "Yeah! And he said you jacked him up for his money and we had to give his mother twenty cents that you took from him. We didn't raise you to be a gangster. And as soon as you put your foot back in the door you're gonna get it!"

My uncles and aunts were boiling with disgust. I didn't want them to become more enraged but I just had to say something in my defense. "I didn't take one penny from Earl. When I got to the store he was playing the pinball machine. Then he left, and I played a game."

I pleaded and swore, but I couldn't tell if they believed me or not. I finally got a chance to tell my aunt that the storekeeper didn't have the brand she wanted. She stared at me for a moment and said "Go back and get Lucky Strikes."

My uncle reiterated "And when you get back, we're beatin' yo' ass! Get outta here and hurry back!"

Well, that certainly didn't please me. The thought of my uncle striking me made me terribly upset because he had never hit me before. Just a trip to the store had now turned into a nightmare. I left the house once again heading for the store, quite bewildered. The promise from my uncle echoed over and over; "...and when you get back... and when you get back...."

They are going to kill me, I thought to myself. I was so scared. When I

14

got back to the store, I explained what had happened to the storekeeper.

He said, "I saw Earl spend his money in the pinball machine, and I'll tell your folks what happened if you want me to." I was relieved to hear him say that. I did at least know that I wasn't crazy. That explanation wouldn't help my case, because my aunts and uncles were buried inside and were not about to come out in the snow to hear anyone's testimony. I paid for the cigarettes and began walking back home. My body shivered with fear. I was terrified and decided I needed divine intervention. So, right there, I looked up to the big bright moon and knelt down in the snow next to some steps and began praying. "God please, please, don't let them whip me. You know that I didn't take that boy's money. Please let them believe me, please God. If you do this for me, I will always remember you answered my prayer and I will always trust you."

That was the most monumental prayer I ever prayed in my life that I can remember. I convinced myself that if there was a God in heaven, he wouldn't allow my folks to follow through with their promise. I got up off my knees and went home. I gave my aunt the cigarettes and no one said a word about the incident. It was like it never happened. I made sure that I didn't get in anyone's way, and stayed very quiet. I counted this as a heavenly miracle accompanied by a heavenly message. After several years, I asked them about the incident and they couldn't even remember it.

I never forgot it and it had a lot to do with how I perceived my relationship with God, even today. God gave me the instant help that I needed and played a major role in guiding my footsteps throughout my life.

I attended Robert Vaux Jr. High School. I knew early on I wouldn't like it. My best friends were Joe Smith, and my cousins Ernest and Elner 'Diddie' Greer. They lived at 21st and Burkes across the street from the pool hall. It was about a fifteen minute walk from my house on Arlington Street. Ernest was a jazz buff. He always kept his collection updated and had what made his vinyl the neighborhood's best. We had good clean fun. Alcohol and drugs were not part of our lives. Joe was a body-builder whose muscles were buffed good enough to compete in body-building competitions. I wasn't quite that good, but I wasn't bashful about wearing a tight tee shirt. We went to school every day in spite of the fact we didn't really like it. The counselor wanted to enroll me in auto mechanics. That just wasn't me. So rather than change oil and fix flats, I was out of there. I detested the idea of getting my hands and nails all filled with grease and oil. I wanted to be a banker, a business owner or a musician.

I usually had a job, nice clothes, and kept an impressive amount of money in my pocket as a teenager. I was noted to be a suave dresser because I was slim and looked good in my threads. Moreover, I had good taste and was capable of setting trends. Some of the guys would check me out, and then go shopping.

When I attended dances at the Reynolds Hall, I was usually one of the best dressed there. I was quite a 'dapper' from head to toe, and had awesome dancing ability that the girls loved.

Bob Montgomery, the boxing champ, had a pool hall on the corner of 21st and Berke. The Montgomery family was known around Philadelphia because of Bob. This was one of our favorite hangouts. We would shoot pool for hours and hours. Some of the skills I learned then, I still flaunt today. There were very few guys that could beat me. Motown's great Tammi Terrell was Bob Montgomery's niece. Her real name was Tammie Montgomery. We never saw very much of her because only guys frequented the pool hall. Sometimes she would drop by to see her uncle, but would soon be on her way. So we just got a glimpse of her coming or leaving. She was very pretty and her family kept close tabs on her.

Drugs didn't have a place at all in my circle of friends. I can remember when we first heard whispers that 'Charlie' had some dope. He appeared to be a nice guy on the outside, but his ultimate goal was to sell his wares...marijuana, with the code name 'Vaunce'. In the neighborhood, he would pull out a joint from his watch pocket, and announce, "It's time to get vaunced." This impressed some, because this guy was sharp and super cool. I might have tried it but he placed the joint in his mouth and wet it with his saliva to make it burn slowly. This was a major turn off. I couldn't smoke anything that had been passed around or spat on. Another thing: the ones that did try it would start coughing uncontrollably. So, after putting those factors together, I stayed on the clean side and that was the end of my 'Vaunce' career.

Around 1949, one of my favorite places was the Earl Theater, located on South Street in South Philadelphia. Since I was born May 18, 1934, I would be about fifteen years old. I would forsake all other happenings to be at this spot every Saturday. I made it my business to get there early in order to get a front row seat. The place would be packed like sardines in a can. After all, there were three events – a movie, comedy show, and live music. Some of the performers were Pigmeat Markham and Lionel Hampton.

I enjoyed the entire package, but I was profoundly impressed with the vibe playing of Lionel Hampton. I had never seen anyone play the vibes with so much energy and fluency. It was like watching a magician. His moves seemed impossible, but the melodic flow of sounds from his instrument captured me, and I was hooked instantly. When the lights focused on those big golden vibes, I perceived that instrument as the prettiest I had ever seen. My fate was sealed and I wanted to play 'Midnight Sun' right then and there, just as Lionel had. In order to just saturate my soul, I would remain through several shows to see those golden vibes and to treat my ears to Hampton's heavenly sounds.

Around 1952 we moved from Arlington Street to 27th Street. I hated leaving the old 'hood' but my folks found a better place and it was time to go. The adjustment period was very short lived. Immediately, I met some other cats that were aspiring musicians as well. James Hilley played trumpet and Joe King was a sensational conga drum player, and I provided the vibes. We would play for hours at a time. The instrumentation wasn't the usual mix, but we were not encumbered. Joe King's career escalated with many opportunities offered to him from the big name acts. I didn't own a set of vibes at this time, but I was working on a job with my brother to save the money for at least a down payment.

I acquired this job through divine order. The way things happened made me feel I was on God's list of special people, and pretty close to the top. This was a welding job, and in order to be accepted the requirement was to simply pass a welding test. That sounds simple enough, if you are a competent welder. I had a knowledge. The task had to be performed with perfection but mine had a small flaw that really should have been marked failed. I held my breath as the test examiner looked over my work and marked my test as 'PASSED'.

"God, you are awesome." I had a flashback to the night I prayed in the snow. I proclaimed this to be yet another miracle. I just knew that I had failed because I could see the imperfection in the job, but the examiner's eyes had become sightless. I worked every day and couldn't wait to make the purchase of my life – a set of vibes. As much as I loved clothes, this didn't even matter now the vibes had priority over everything. I hadn't established credit and I wasn't patient enough to buy

17

on the lay-away plan so my brother said he would co-sign for me.

Before those words left his mouth good, we were at the Wurlitzer Company, downtown on Chestnut Street in Philadelphia. I'll never forget the moment I cast my eyes upon that 510 Performer vibes. It was a beauty! I must have been smiling from ear to ear, I felt that I was at the pinnacle of my heart's desires. I was happy, happy, happy. That purchase meant I had successfully crossed a prestigious hurdle in my life. The next hurdle was to abort my amateurish dabbling and become a professional musician. I could play anything I heard and I had 'good ears'. I managed to jam a few times on stage with some of the local cats around Philadelphia. Carl Bell was my mailman and also a drummer who had a trio. He heard me play a few times and approached me about playing with him. "My vibe player quit on me the other night. How would you like to come and be a regular with us, four nights a week?" he asked.

The question paralyzed me and I mumbled, "Four nights a week?"

Carl thought that I was inferring it was too much and I had a problem with the amount of days. "We can work something out, but I sure would like for you to take the gig, because I like the way you play," he pleaded.

"No, no, the four days will be just fine." I wasn't about to turn this gig down. What he didn't know was I would have taken a one nighter with him. I was flattered that he even asked me.

James Pringle was on organ, Garland Smith played saxophone, Carl Bell played drums and Billy Paul ('Me and Mrs. Jones' Billy Paul) was the performing vocalist. This was great, night after night. It was a local bar, but we kept the place packed. I was still living on 27th Street with my mom and aunts. My uncles had either moved out or they were married. Some of my family members would sometimes come to hear me play. My brother Al was most supportive and would stop by with his police friends very often

In between practicing and playing at the club, I had a little time to date. I had my eyes on a young lady who lived next door, named Peggy White. It was literally next door because we lived in what were called 'row' houses and, with just a couple of steps, I was next door.

My Aunt Ernesta was a beautician. Peggy would often come over to have her hair curled. I would find every excuse to be at home when she came over. I loved to just watch her because she was so nice and so pretty. Her skin was like creamy milk chocolate, her teeth were pearly white, her legs were perfectly shaped and she had an hour glass figure.

I'm sure that every guy in the neighborhood dreamed of her because she was as close to perfect as anyone could have been. I had the advantage over the other guys because I lived right next door. We found romance and dated for a little less than a year.

I proposed and Miss Peggy White became Mrs. Peggy Ashford. I was twenty and she was twenty-one years old. I wasn't able to lease an apartment for us, so I moved next door with Peggy and her cousin. With making about a dozen steps, I had moved into my in-laws' house with my new bride. There would be several moves after this one. One move was with one of my uncles and eventually we lived alone. During that time I was traveling with Carl Bell's Band, which proved to be a costly problem to our marriage. I didn't want the marriage to end, so I began seeking local job opportunities with other bands. I was fortunate to become a part of Jimmy Garrison's Jazz Group. I also played with a pick up group from New York who had Johnny Hammond Smith, (organ) Leo Stevens, (drums) and Eddie McFadden, (guitar) and I played vibes.

My marriage was back on track and I was working steadily in town.

And then the inevitable. A letter from my Uncle...Sam that is. The year was 1958, and I was at the tender age of 24. "Greetings from the President of the United States." The letter included instructions to 'bring enough clothes for three days'. It didn't sink in what this letter really meant. I didn't take the clothes because I had no plans for staying over. I was sure that I would be returning to my wife that evening. That morning, when I responded to the letter, I kissed my wife goodbye and stated firmly that I would be seeing her that evening after work. Upon my arrival at the induction center, I was given a battery of tests. The examiner escorted me to a room crammed with other males and we waited for the results.

I wondered why I had to wait. I would have been very happy to receive the results in the mail.

An Army official appeared and announced: "You have all passed the test and you will now be inducted into the military." This has to be some kind of prank or this guy is a real lunatic.

"Uh Sir, excuse me, but did you say we-will-now-be-inducted-into-the-military?" I cried.

Without even acknowledging me, or my question he announced, "Take one step forward, and raise your right hand please." About a hundred other men and I complied, and were sworn together to serve our country.

"You're now in the United States Army," roared the officer.

August 12, 1958, had certainly changed my life. I felt overwhelmed, weak, dismayed, depressed and defenseless. There was nothing to insulate me from Uncle Sam's twenty-four month plan. I thought maybe soon someone would awake me and tell me I was having a bad dream. Instead, an officer announced "The bus is here to take you soldiers to Fort Eustis, Virginia."

I became comatose. I couldn't speak, but it wouldn't have done any good anyway. After arriving at Fort Eustis, I called to inform my wife and mom of my new job. "Hello Honey, you can never guess where I am, and I won't be coming home for dinner," I blurted out in one breath.

She said. "I don't want to try and guess, please explain!"

"I'm in the United States Army, and I didn't even enlist. They drafted me! Let Mom know." I think she dropped the phone, she was just as surprised as I was.

That first night I caught hell trying to sleep. I wrestled with the reality of events that had taken place. I was in a total quandary and there was absolutely nothing I could do about it. The words 'You're now in the United States Army' reverberated over and over again. It didn't take long for me to conclude that I hated the army. I had problems adjusting and was sent to a psychiatrist who recommended I be given a position of authority. This turned out to be a workable proposal. I became a platoon guide and excelled in this position because I really liked it. Once, as a platoon guide, I was appointed to do guard duty and was selected as a 'Supernumerary' (that is a soldier that doesn't march and is held in reserve in case someone else can't perform). To qualify as a Supernumerary, a soldier had to be the neatest dressed, with shined shoes, shined belt buckles, and everything looking like new. I was a natural at dressing and looking 'sharp' so being named Supernumerary didn't surprise anyone. I was never a part of the 'Motley Crew', even as a teenager. This set a precedent for my later diversity.

At the end of basic training, it was graduation time. I was sitting in the ceremony ready to applaud the achievements of other soldiers when I heard my name called. "Jack Ashford, the highest scorer of the proficiency test." My jaw dropped. I was called to the stage to receive my trophy. Several other awards were given as the ceremony advanced. It was now time for the final award. I seemed to have been glued to my seat when I heard the officer announce: "This trophy is given to the most outstanding soldier, Pvt. Jack Ashford." Well, certainly not me, there must be two of us with the same name. I was still sitting, looking for this other Jack Ashford. It hit me like a bolt of lightning from the blue. The announcement meant out of all the trainees from this particular cycle, I was the most outstanding soldier. I stood, and it was evident that the element of surprise had practically swept me off my feet. The other soldiers gave me a round of thunderous applause.

I didn't like the Army at first, but after I faced the truth and accepted the military seriously, I applied myself and became a great soldier.

After graduation, there were more orders. I was assigned to Fort Houston, Virginia, the transportation capital of the military. My first assignment was to a boat company. This meant I would have to tour Thule, Greenland.

To me, that was the coldest spot in the world. It was even too cold for Eskimos. I knew I had to put on my thinking cap and try to avoid going there. I said to one of the officers, "I can't go there. I don't mind cold weather, but Thule, Greenland is totally preposterous. Do they have people living there?"

He looked at me and said "If your orders say go to Thule, I'm a hundred per cent sure you'll go to Thule."

We had a couple of days off and headed to Virginia. We were given an explanation of future duties of the soldiers going to Thule. Instead of me listening like a good soldier, I asked a sergeant, "Is there any way I can get out of going to Greenland?"

He said "Yeah, but you won't be able to do it." I wanted to know why not. He explained, "The only way to get out of going is that you gotta be sick, or your wife has got to be sick, and the only guy I know of that got out of Greenland duty went to the Marksmanship Board."

I pondered for a moment because I wasn't familiar with that branch of the service. "Ummm, Marksmanship Board, what is that?"

"That means you're selected to be a shooter on the Rifle Team or The Pistol Team and you represent the United States in shooting competitions."

Very interesting! I always had the gift to shoot and hearing those words gave me a glimmer of hope. This could very well be my ticket away from Greenland.

I remember when I was a kid we would take thirty caliber bullets to the park and put them into the ground with the tips pointing to the ground on a hill. I would take a Bee-Bee rifle and stand about twenty feet away, fire at the primer, hit it and discharge the shell into the ground. Another example of my shooting ability was how I could shoot mice and kill them with one shot using a Bee-Bee rifle.

I pursued the conversation and pumped the sergeant to find out more about getting on the Rifle Team. The Sergeant said, "There's a company competition, where soldiers compete against each other, and as you ascend through the process and make it to the finals, you will then be eligible to compete for a position."

A few days passed and the Commanding Officer did call for men to compete. When he asked for volunteers, my hand went up like it had a spring on it. My hand went up first. My request was approved and I went to the shooting competition and out-scored everybody in my squad. After that I beat everybody in my company. The next competition was to shoot against all of the other soldiers on the post. Out of all the soldiers that had fired that day, I was ranked number three. There were maybe two hundred shooting that day. Go Jack! I gave myself an A plus for confidence and A plus for actually making the team. Likely, some of the guys going to Greenland were envious, but kept their feelings subdued. My name was submitted as a candidate on the Rifle Team.

Two weeks later there was a formation of my company to announce who would be going to Greenland. Most of the soldiers were dreading what they were about to hear, but I was all smiles. The sergeant announced: "I'm going to read the names of the soldiers that are not going to Greenland from this Company. There's only one name (he paused), and that is – Private Jack Ashford."

Hallelujah! This story may sound like one of those fairy tales from the wooded forest, but this is a true account of what happened. This is just another one of God's miracles in my life.

I reported to the Marksmanship Board. Out of twenty-five soldiers, I was the only African American. When I first entered the room, shock was written all over their faces. My presence was comparable to a cannon being shot into the room. The men were from the mid-west and from the south. The sergeant congratulated me, but the other men were not beaming with joy because they knew to be on the same shooting team meant a lot of sharing. We traveled extensively, participating in several competitions. Our racial differences never became a problem. The men respected me and never judged me because of my skin color but admired me for my trophy-winning ability. There were a couple of soldiers that really looked out for me and protected me from 'harm's way'.

HELLO AGAIN WORLD

I was an outstanding soldier. That fact wasn't a disputable fact. I had souvenirs (trophies) to prove my achievements. I never considered choosing the army as a career, but I did a great job. My mom taught me, whatever job I worked on, to do my best, and that's exactly what I did. I left several friends in the army that retired there, but this just wasn't my kind of work. On August 11, 1960, I returned home after spending two years with Uncle Sam. This day marked one of the happiest days of my life. I was very glad to be a part of the outside world again.

After I was officially discharged, I rode back to Philly with two other friends. We had shared a ride back to Philadelphia several times on a two-day pass, but this time, we were out of the army for good. In spite of celebrating all the way to Philadelphia, the ride seemed like an eternity before we reached the city limits. We reminisced about the vanished yesterdays of army life and how we had managed to endure the rigid routines and lifestyle the army had imposed upon us. "I'm gonna eat the biggest hoagie sandwich I can find." "I'm gonna have the biggest breakfast with scrapple (that's an eastern ground pork/meal dish...), and a dozen eggs." The promises about what we were going to do once we returned home went on and on. As long as I didn't have to stand in line to get my food it didn't matter too much what it was, as long as we were not in the military mess hall. We expressed how much we would miss each other, but would always keep in touch. (One of the guys kept true to his word and we remained close friends.)

Mile by mile, and minute by minute, my heart grew warm with anticipation of seeing my family and my wife. Finally, the view ahead revealed the gray, gloomy outline of the city I called home. Nothing had really changed. The usual daily hustle and bustle of catching the 'el train', or seeing people gather the morning paper and milk from their doorsteps was just a daily routine for people that lived in the third largest city in the US.

I made it home, and my family warmly received me as I shared a lot of 'war stories'.

The hugs, kisses, and slaps on the back confirmed they were all glad to see me. The visionary romantic moments I had dreamed of with my wife were about to become a reality. She was a beautiful woman, who now

24

looked even better than ever. As we tasted of each other's passion, both Venus and Cupid stood guard and shut out the rest of the world, while we tried to make up for lost time.

My first few weeks back were spent just readjusting to civilian life, and being a husband again. Peggy welcomed me home with open arms, but I could feel us growing apart soon after. There were many times when she would just stare into the distance and I would have to escort her back to the moment. She acted very reserved and our conversations were mostly one-sided with me doing most of the talking. The years I spent playing and traveling, and then two years with the army had eaten away at her feelings for me and she was afraid of being left alone again. She explained to me having a husband away from her all the time wasn't what she wanted. Her dream of a good husband was to have a man who worked every day on a job and came home routinely at the same time to have dinner with his wife and kids. With music so deeply embedded in my bones, there's no way I could be that guy. I didn't want to make a choice between her and music, but it turned out that way. I had to play music. That's what I could do well and loved it. I understood how she felt, but I couldn't forfeit my career.

Before leaving for the army I had opened a fish store located on 21st and Ridge Ave. We served a variety of fish and crab meals along with chicken and potato salad. The customers would be lined up to buy Mom's delectable fish cakes. She supplied all of the recipes while me and my friends Autry Harmon and Peanut (I can't remember Peanut's real name) prepared the food, waited on customers, and did the cooking. The place was very small, so the orders were carry-out only. We were very successful as long as I was around. When I was inducted into the army, the business really suffered and almost went under. Peanut didn't have good business skills and the store stayed in the red. Peanut left and the store began experiencing profits again. By now, the entire operation had been crippled by wrong decisions and it was hard to recover. When I returned home the business was hanging on by a thread. I made several attempts to revive the clientele, but after Mom had limited the store hours to just two days per week we lost a lot of our customers. I decided that my time would be better spent doing what I loved best and that was playing vibes.

I started practicing again daily, using every spare moment to sharpen my skills and techniques. I played a little in service, but not quite enough to keep my 'chops up' where they should have been. Spending many hours practicing also encroached upon intimate moments with my wife. The same circumstances that distressed our marriage were being mirrored as I worked rapidly back into playing music. And that was like a triggering mechanism that hurled our marriage into a dark pit of hopelessness and broken dreams. There was no compromise. There was no solution.

"Peggy," I vowed, "I'll always love you and I'll always be here when you need me." Unselfishly she whispered: "Just go, do what you have to do, I'll be alright." I held her closely and wiped away the tears that streamed down her face. Leaving her was like cutting down a beautiful forest to make way for a new housing development. I just prayed that her disappointments would not grow into feelings of hopelessness. This was not the end of the world and, in time, I thought, we could one day reunite and rekindle our affection.

I contacted Carl Bell again. His band had broken up and he was interested in forming a new group. He told me he had an organ player and he had a place for us to practice. He said we could make this a success if I agreed to accept his offer. Carl explained "We will have to practice a lot and my friend Richard 'Groove' Holmes says that we can practice at the place where he works."

I thought about it for a moment and said: "Cool, we can do that."

"Well, we'll have to drive thirty-five miles to Jersey, is that O.K.?" Carl asked.

"That's fine", I quickly answered. Carl never told me where 'Groove' worked. I didn't have an inkling of an idea that he worked at a funeral home until we arrived there for our first get-acquainted rehearsal. When Carl pulled over and parked, I didn't move a muscle. I simply resumed my relaxed, reclined, position.

Carl inquired, "Well aren't you going to get out?"

"For what? Are we gonna rehearse with some 'dead beats'?" I jokingly asked.

"Naw, man, this is where Richard works and can rehearse here because they have an organ. Bring your vibes and come on," Carl insisted. I got out and rolled my vibes in by way of the back door where dead bodies were prepared. This horrendous scene almost paralyzed me. I didn't want to appear to be a wimp, but my experience with the dead was strictly at funerals and very few of them. As we walked through the morbid little prep room, we passed by a table that had a dead body on it. Richard pulled back the rubber sheet back to expose the corpse. I was looking right down into the man's open chest cavity. I became ill and near death after that myself. Richard proudly explained, "Now that brother had to have an autopsy, and...."

I rudely interrupted, "OK, but we're not interested right now. Are we Carl?" Richard just laughed, because he detected my nervousness. We went to the chapel where the organ was, and began rehearsing. I continued to have flashbacks and the rehearsal turned out to be a flop for me. I just couldn't shake the image of the corpse. After that day, the next rehearsals were much better, but I never grew fond of the funeral home, and I wouldn't ever shake Richard's hand. He had a lot of episodes and tales to share about the 'stiffs'. Carl took pleasure in hearing some of Richard's accounts, but he knew I only wanted to hear about the living.

The Carl Bell Trio played at many of the local bars for several months. When one gig was terminated, we were immediately ready for the next job. Getting jobs was not a problem because there was a bar almost on every corner. We worked continuously, and actually had a following. James Prangle, our next organist, would quite often flirt from the stage with pretty ladies. Some took him seriously while others knew he was a playful guy. He wasn't a real good looking guy, but the ladies just seemed to be attracted to him. Carl was the kind of guy that was serious about getting the job done in order to get paid. He would often warn us that "The women are out there and they'll come right up to the stage and get you. So, be careful." These ladies are now called groupies, but back then they were called something else.

Carl owned a beautiful 1949 convertible Buick that he always parked right in front of the club. Many times after gigging we would pile into his car with the top back and just ride around the city. We were all nocturnal and enjoyed visiting some of the other night spots that were still open. It was that or we would have a four o'clock breakfast. Nobody had a car but Carl, so he always took us home after playing.

James got another job with another band. Carl tried to find another organ player but his efforts were ineffectual. With me, I was pretty lucky. After less than a week or two, I found work with The Charles Harris Trio. We worked several of the local clubs and bars. And here again we had our own following. Our trio was known around town as having a good solid jazz sound. The way we blended complimented each other and we came off as real pros. The word spread up to the Eastern seaboard that we were crowd pleasers and could boost any club's business. In time, Charles began getting calls from out of town club owners. "What would you guys think of going to New York or Boston to work?" Charles inquired. This really surprised me. We were doing well in Philadelphia and Charles hadn't given us any indication that he was anticipating a job move. We appeared somewhat stunned for a minute and then total silence. "What's wrong? Are you guys scared to leave Philly? What do you have to keep you here?" He blasted the questions one after the other.

I spoke first. "Will the money be any better? 'cause if we aren't paid anymore, I see no need to hit the road."

Charles sincerely explained "The money is much better and we have a chance to travel the coast. It's no telling who we'll run into, but I really feel like we have to get out of Philly."

Chi-Ching! "OK, I see your point and I agree that this is what we should do. Let's do it."

The three of us made plans to get out on the road. Charles had confirmed our first job in Boston and we immediately began packing and getting ready. In about two weeks we arrived in Boston. The bar owner kept his promise that he would reserve a nice comfortable hotel room for us. What he didn't say was that two of us would have to share a room. As much as I hated sharing a room, it worked out alright. Quite a few jazz recording artists would drop in on our shows. We played very well together and made it a point to play the tunes that were recorded by the guests when they dropped by to see us perform. They appreciated that recognition.

The audiences loved us in Boston as much as they did in Philadelphia. We played in several clubs in Boston and later traveled to Lansing, Michigan to work there. The club atmosphere in Lansing was somewhat different. There weren't many clubs there, and the town became almost paralyzed after midnight. That's because it was a small college town and quite different from the eastern cities. Everybody knew everybody, and there were very few secrets. I remember there was a tall, freckled-face pretty lady that came to the club two or three times a week and would always sit near the bandstand. She flaunted her curves and other parts of her sensational anatomy.

I shared a few intermissions with her, and one night she invited me to dinner the following Sunday at her apartment. Carl Bell's words impacted my mind like a speeding locomotive, "BE CAREFUL!"

This lady's beauty had me almost in a spell and I didn't heed Carl's warning at all. "Will your boyfriend be there too?" I asked that question to find out if she had a boyfriend. She quickly spoke as though I had really insulted her, "Boyfriend? I don't have a boyfriend right now." Those words actually struck me as not being true because she was so fine. But at the same time I couldn't say no.

I simply said "What time Sunday?"

She thought for a minute and said "Oh about three o'clock, will that give you enough time?"

I said "That's perfect, and you're sure you don't have a boyfriend?" She assured me she didn't and dinner would be ready and waiting. I mentioned the dinner date to Charles, and he exclaimed, "Man-n-n, I wouldn't touch that with a ten foot pole. As fine as she is, you know that she has a relationship with somebody!"

Sunday arrived. I dressed real sharp, dapped myself with cologne and caught a cab to what was supposed to be a great dinner and I had plans for the dessert. Out of anticipation, I arrived a little before three. I rang the doorbell and almost instantly she greeted me with a big smile and invited me into her extravagantly furnished apartment. "Nice place you have here" I said, as I scanned the rooms.

"Oh, thank you. Just make yourself at home and come on into the dining room."

About this time, someone started banging on the door. The banging was so loud it sounded like thunder. To myself I thought, "Oh my God!!! Could this be her man?" I asked her, "Who is that knocking on your door?" I couldn't believe her next statement.

"That's a friend of mine that's a policeman. Carl's words and Charles' words became all too clear. I had to find my way out of her place and there was only one door – the front door.

Luckily she lived on the first floor, because I made my exit right out of the window. I didn't see the guy nor did he see me. I hit the ground running and left a trail of dust behind me. When I got to the boulevard I flagged a cab and went back home. I called Charles and told him how right he was. He laughed at me about that dinner date for a long time.

One night when we were really jamming and grooving on stage I happened to look up and notice 'Freckles' was there with a man, and he was constantly looking at me, and then to Charles. He did this several times. He seemed to have been trying to intimidate us. It didn't really matter because the guy didn't know me from anybody else. I learned my lesson that day and never accepted another dinner invitation from a lady.

The band played for a few more weeks and we returned to Boston.

Without foreseeing any sign of a change, destiny aligned us with a very significant sequence of events we had never encountered. As musicians, we were about to embark upon a segment of our careers that would be a providential blessing.

MEETING MOTOWN

In 1963 I was doing what I wanted to be doing. Traveling to near places and not so near places, such as New England, playing jazz and performing swinging gigs. I was living my dream and playing all the hot spots. When I needed another musical gig to pay off, one was there. My involvement got deeper and deeper and I was continuing my love affair with the music.

But, at this point, my life and career was set to take an incredible spin when fate introduced me to destiny.

We were playing Boston. It was a night I thought would be very routine. I lugged my vibes and bag of percussion instruments into the club as always. The setting was a dimly lit, smoke filled, small jazz club, with a stage that was elevated just enough to overlook the crowd. Lights that were somewhat like small Christmas lights dotted the windows here and there. The gloom was broken by typical bar signs and neon lights, advertising beer and other alcoholic drinks. Patrons gathered in the mirrored bar to drink mixers and check out every lady that entered.

On this night, everyone waited anxiously to cut away from the sounds of Coltrane playing on the juke box to those of a live jazz outfit – The Charles Harris Trio. Our trio pumped out all of the latest jazz tunes that were hits at the time.

At last, we were up there playing and I felt we were doing great. After five or six tunes, Charles got us in a huddle like a football team captain and said the audience seemed bored. People were drifting away and, by closing time, there was only a handful left.

As we packed up our instruments in silence, the club owner told us we had one more night to make a better impression, or we'd be replaced.

It didn't look good. But Charles had an idea and next day went over to the music store and bought a tambourine. That night, as we were setting up ready to play, he handed it to me.

"Well?" I said, "What do you want me to do with this?"

He replied in a voice that didn't invite discussion: "Play it!"

I stared at the thing, hoping it might disappear, thinking: I'm a hard-core jazz musician. Tambourines are for black sanctified churches, not night-club stages.

I tried to reason with Charles: "Listen, man, I've never played one of these things and I don't know how."

Charles was a man with a plan and reason didn't come into it: "OK, man. Like I'm trying to do something here to get everybody a bit more excited so we can hold on to this gig."

He sat down at the organ and counted in Dave Brubeck's 'Take Five' – "One-two, One-two-three." He vamped the five-four intro chords and looked right at me with fire in his eyes. "Pick up the tambourine." Then louder and more insistent: "Pick up the tambourine!"

I handled it with disgust and mistrust, but I picked it up and started playing it – or should I say the tambourine started playing itself? It was *so* mystical. I can't explain it. It was in my hands, but like someone else was pounding out the rhythm.

Conversation among the audience halted and the attention was all on us. People even started to move closer to the stage. When the song thundered to an end it was met by an ovation that must have lasted a full two or three minutes.

Charles was all smiles: "I thought you couldn't play the tambourine...."

We went straight into the Latin tune, 'Watermelon Man', and soon the place was really rocking. People picked up the groove from outside and the club started filling up.

When the show was over, the club owner complimented us on the addition of the tambourine and took back his threat to replace us. It was music to our ears to hear that he wanted us to return the next night and indefinitely.

By 'hit' time the next night, the club was standing room only. The word had circulated in the neighborhood that The Charles Harris Trio had a sound that was as different as night and day. The club was packed to capacity with people anxious to treat their ears to something different.

We talked and critiqued the previous night's action but, for fear of breaking the magic, we didn't rehearse. We just talked.

After the first set, we left the stage for a break. As I was stepping down, a guy walked up to me, extended his hand and said: "Hello, I'm John Lockhart." He began telling me about another guy named Marvin Gaye, and pointed him out in the club. I had noticed him earlier because he was wearing a funny-colored suit. He led me over to where Marvin was sitting with his dark green threads and shades and introduced me.

Marvin asked if I had heard any of his records or the company he cut for. I had to tell him I never heard of him, his records or any company.

"What instrument do you play?" I asked him.

"I'm a singer," he told me. Realizing I really was unaware of his latest musical hits, he moved on to the subject of the future. "I think your trio is really great and I just wondered if you guys would be interested in joining me on my US tour." Marvin had a good ear for jazz (obviously). One of his favorite players was a pianist who sometimes went by the name of Shorty Nadine. You and I know him as Nat King Cole.

We really didn't know what to say to Marvin, so Charles exchanged numbers with him, but we really didn't get too excited.

Perhaps a few weeks passed by and we were gigging in my Philadelphia home town. I had bought my mom a house and on this particular day was preparing for a move in when my brother Al stopped by. I was taking advantage of a three day lay off to do some painting.

Al shouted up to me, "Bro', you got a telegram from Detroit." The meeting with Marvin had gone right out of my mind by that time so I was totally surprised by this news. The telegram read: "We will pay your expenses to come to Detroit for a rehearsal with you and members of the band. Please call this number for more information," and it was signed by Marvin Gaye.

I called Charles and he was as surprised as I was. We talked about it for a few minutes and considered our options. It took about that long. I laid down my paint brush, pulled out the atlas and mapped out our best route to Detroit.

We still had a few days left to fulfill our commitment at the club in West Philly, so we decided to conclude all of our business and leave the following weekend.

We filled the tank of the Cadillac hearse – yes, hearse! It was the perfect transport for organ groups. During that time, organs were the instruments of choice, à la Jimmy Smith and 'Groove' Holmes.

So we headed toward Detroit on this odyssey and tried to imagine what we were in for. But after jazz we didn't have a clue. We saw ourselves as hard-core jazzmen and didn't recognize any other kind of music. As we drove to Detroit, we pictured Marvin as some kind of Big Band Count Basie type and saw us touring with him for six or seven months. We had no idea just how popular Marvin really was.

The drive to Detroit was somewhat exhausting, to put it mildly. We stopped at a few places to eat, but slept in the hearse. It didn't matter much. We just wanted to get there. And, believe it or not, ours wasn't the only hearse on the highway not carrying 'stiffs'. We saw quite a few like ours carrying musical instruments.

We talked and laughed until our conversation drifted off into personal thoughts and everything went quiet, except for the motor and the tires humming. The constant sound of motion acted as a hypnotic spell. My eyes became heavy and sleep was inevitable. I was in a deep sleep (probably snoring) when Charles shook me: "Jack, Jack! We're heading for a tornado. It's forming up ahead and the cars are pulling under the overpass on both sides."

Naturally, I woke up crazy and couldn't believe what I was hearing. Charles pulled over. I looked out in the field, maybe seventy-five yards away, and saw a lady with a baby in her arms. She was coming from a farmhouse and yelling for help. Everyone was holed up in their cars and no one could hear her.

Before I knew it, I jumped out of the car and over the fence. I ran over to help her. She was quite distressed. She said: "Thank God. Thank God for you," and handed me the baby so she could retain her grip on a strong box she was carrying.

By this time, the wind was really buffeting us around. We labored to get to the fence by the highway because the wind was very strong and powerful. I wasn't able to help her over the fence. Instead, I held the baby and the strong box.

After several tries, she made it completely over the fence and on to a car where the occupants welcomed her by opening the door. She got in the car and thanked me over and over.

I was pushed back one step for every two attempts, but I made it back to the hearse. As I made the comparative safety of the interior, the angry wind slammed trash and debris against the outside.

Eventually, a calm settled. The woman and her child were gone, never to be seen by me again, and the storm was as if it had never been. We pressed on to our last overnight stop.

When the sun rose on Sunday morning, we were within a hundred miles of the Detroit city limits. A couple of hours later, we were on John C. Lodge Expressway and into West Grand Boulevard. We anticipated a long drive off the expressway but after exiting from this big tree-lined island street, we were soon looking at 2648 West Grand Boulevard, still with no idea that this address would one day be famous throughout the world.

It was a cool, crisp fall morning and there were a lot of cars parked near the studio. Fortunately for us, there was one space we could squeeze the hearse into. Ironically, it was right in front of Cole's Funeral Home, which was right next door to the house that called itself 'Hitsville', and unknown to us at that time would serve a double purpose as a refuge for overworked musicians in the decade to come.

This 'Hitsville' didn't look like any company headquarters. It looked like a flat. We walked up the sidewalk and on to the porch. There was a big picture window that displayed some of the 'Motown' artists' pictures. I had never heard of any of them – Mary Wells, Stevie Wonder and others – though they were clearly popular and hot on the charts.

We stood and listened for a moment. I said to Charles, "Hey, man. I hear some music playing, but no lights are on in the lobby."

So Charles said, "Well, somebody's in there. Knock on the door."

I knocked, but no one answered. I then started to *bang* on the door, harder and harder. Finally, a little short guy came to the door and spoke in an assuring tone. "May I please help you?"

I started complaining: "I've been knocking on this door for fifteen minutes. You need a doorbell!" I rattled on at him, but the little guy seemed not to be shaken or disturbed by me. "I'm here to see Marvin Gaye. He sent me and my friend a telegram to come down and see him. Is he here?"

He said: "Oh, yes. He told me about you guys. He's here. Come on in." We stepped into the lobby which, at that time, had a l-o-o-o-n-g, loud, orange leather couch pushed next to the window.

Little did I know it, I had just entered the building that would help to shape my musical career in a tremendous way. I was at the point of meeting Motown and getting acquainted with the 'family'. Still less did I realise I had just been talking to the founder and owner, Berry Gordy, Jr.

I thought there would be just another gig at the end of it, but it would be a world away from all that. How could I know that this meeting with Marvin and his brother-in-law, Harvey Fuqua – and his other brother-in-law, Berry Gordy – would transform my future?

Many people now are interested in what the studio looked like and how it was engineered. Moreover, others constantly ask about the camaraderie of the 'Motown Family'. I recall that first visit as if it were yesterday and carry the sense of that family with me forever.

There was a control room with a kind of console. It was very narrow and about six feet deep and eight feet wide. Off to the left of that there was a restroom. To the right was the tape library. Nearby, a pair of stairs led to the basement, which held the supplies. This was the territory of 'Ptomaine Annie', the resident housekeeper who also sold sandwiches.

As we approached the control room, the sound really became loud.

This area was like a vestibule. We stepped into another hallway, which was about five feet by four. Berry opened the door and we stepped for the first time into 'the Snakepit', where there was a window on the left facing the control booth and, once again, another door. It seemed like a tour of a never-ending maze.

In the sunken room, which had been a converted garage, music filled the building. The room was overflowing with members of the Motown Family. Smokey Robinson, Stevie Wonder and even photographers were crammed into this space resembling a beehive.

Scanning the studio, I got my first sight of Earl Van Dyke on piano, Robert White (guitar), James Jamerson (bass), Bennie Benjamin (drums), Joe Messina (guitar) Clarence Paul (sax) and a few other musicians Marvin had contacted.

Actually, it was a Stevie Wonder session. The studio was packed, but these guys were accustomed to playing in those cramped conditions. Maybe that was the magic of it all.

After the handshaking, introductions and smalltalk, I heard Clarence say: "Let's do a safety, so Marvin can get in here with his band." Once more, little did I know that I was sitting with some of the guys that would ultimately become one of the hottest recording rhythm sections in the history of music.

I remember the impression so strongly from that time. The studio was so overwhelmingly small. Because it was so compact and brimming with people, the crowdedness could not be ignored. People were literally jammed into it. Maybe this is what made the music so tight. This atmosphere made the sessions so informal because of the physical closeness.

The focal point of the studio, and looking all the more enormous in that tiny room, was the big Steinway piano.

But, for all that, the studio was very much ahead of its time. Motown had a unique intercom system, which used a microphone hanging from the ceiling. When I first saw it, I was intrigued and inquired about the purpose of that location for the mike.

I was told it was there to enable Berry to communicate with the musicians and those in the control room from his office on the second floor, next to the A&R (artists and repertoire) department.

Right then a lot of things seemed puzzling, but one thing was very clear to us. Diamonds, fine clothes, big cars and the signs of success were all around.

On that first visit, the musicians were cutting a song, and the reason I was there was to also make my mark in the world of R&B. When the sessions were over, Marvin and Harvey showed up along with other musicians from various parts of the country that Marvin had told to come to Detroit for this meeting.

As I evaluate that incident now, it was nothing but an audition to find out how large the band would be and how long it would take to get them ready for the road. Marvin said that a tour of America with the band was about to begin. He also said that it would include a lot of one-nighters and would demand high energy of the players.

Excitement was brewing from within and I was set for a tour that would be filled with excitement, and prove to be part of a series of life transforming events that would live forever.

WHAT IS THE MOTOWN SOUND?

Much of what you hear on the records is the personality of the musicians bleeding through the tracks. No one producer or even group of producers could have instructed us to do exactly what we did on those tracks. As studio musicians, we brought life to what the producers had written on the charts. The success of Motown was dependent upon the geniuses of its musicians who interpreted the ideas and creations of the writers, arrangers, and producers. Then as musicians we embellished that. Berry Gordy was the driving force of this unique company that seemed to have overpowered much of the music that existed in the early sixties and replaced it with what was known all over the world as 'The Motown Sound'. Competitors made futile attempts to analyze and dissect Motown tracks.

The question, "What is the Motown sound?" has been asked by the music audience probably more than any other in the music business. The question hasn't been totally laid to rest but people still have debatable theories. Some have said that the Motown sound was characterized by James Jamerson's dominating bass line, Earl's thunder on the piano, Benny Benjamin's drum pick ups, or even my rocking sanctified tambourines. The Motown sound was not created by any one producer, one writer, one arranger, or one musician. It was the combination of musicians blending and synchronizing their instruments to give birth to an immortal style of music

These musicians were actually jazz musicians who found it easier to make a living recording in studios and working in the club circuit at night. Millions loved the tracks we laid down, but our names were anonymous. We were the Funk Brothers.

I challenge you to listen to a Motown track and try to imagine the main player being only the bass player James Jamerson, or the only player Uriel Jones on drums. What do you have other than solo tracks? And solo tracks can't paint the whole picture. I salute the legendary talents of James Jamerson and Bennie Benjamin, but it required all of us to create the Motown sound.

I can't take anything from the artists, they were sensational, but our music orchestrated the magic in making legendary hits – hits that will live forever.

Robert White and Jamerson would often clash. They had monumental arguments most of the time. They would toss names back and forth at each other. I think much of the contention was provoked by the idea that Jamerson was picking up an extra check from Berry and Robert didn't like that at all. In fact nobody liked it but we didn't show our resentment. The arguments were usually initiated by Robert. He would often scold Jamerson for drinking.

This VIP treatment was probably designed to keep the musicians feuding and preventing us from really uniting as we should have. With constant upheavals, we were not all closely bonded and could be controlled better. None of this would affect the quality of our music. Robert practiced martial arts and was good at it. Jamerson knew a few moves, but was in no way a match for Robert.

We never toured as the Funk Brothers and we never had a release in our name, but we were the hottest band of R&B.

I remember when we received only $10 per tune. You didn't just have an optical illusion while reading. You read correctly – $10, or ten big ones. It was after the death of Bennie that we started getting scale pay. (No connection to his death.) We joined the Detroit Musicians Union at this time.

In the early sixties, $10 a tune was slave labor. During that time we were loyal and had a burning desire to work. We needed the money, but it never became an issue. Eventually the Funk Brothers bonded very closely.

We never saw skin color and we always recognized each other's talents without jealousy or malice. After all we were paid the same salary.

Well, that depends on who was doing the talking. One report was Berry secretly had side deals with James Jamerson and Earl Van Dyke. I hadn't heard about Earl's deal until after his death. That's how secretive it was. Earl probably exhausted all of his 'side deal money' chasing down Bennie and Jamerson for sessions.

After we grew close, I don't think the brotherhood that existed between the Funks was comparable to any other group in the industry. We looked out for each other in and away from the studio. I can remember times when Bennie would go off the loose end and couldn't be found at the time of the session. One of us would go and find him and get him to the studio. Bob Babbitt and Joe Messina were our Caucasian brothers.

We cared absolutely nothing about color. Our common interest was music and brotherhood. Joe Messina was one of the several 'Joes' around Motown, but very distinguishable by his character and concern for others. Joe was about the nicest guy that you could ever meet and twice as talented. Bob was the emotional one of the group. His kind and tender spirit would be touched often as we talked about tough times, or times we shared. He too was a very nice guy that would give you his last dollar if you needed it.

Back to the Motown sound and what it is. If you fully examine the tracks you may understand the key elements that went into each recording. It's also important to understand that it wasn't just Jamerson's sound that other musicians were trying to duplicate, it was every Funk Brother's contribution that went into the completion of every track. Each musician played an indispensable role.

The 'real experts' said that the equipment had to be the answer to making hits, so they would overhaul their consoles or purchase new ones for their studios. Some felt it was the Motown engineers, while others felt it was the dimensions of the Snake Pit (Studio A). Some wanted to take a look at the wooden floors to see what kind of wood the floors were made of. There were so many asinine and dumb impressions.

Most people overlooked the simple truth and essential element – The Funk Brothers.

Musicians made feverish attempts to dissect the drum sound, never realizing that there were three drummers. They were Bennie Benjamin, Uriel Jones and Richard 'Pistol' Allen. Bennie provided some sensational pick-ups that pleasured every drummer's ears and gave them something to try to duplicate. The drum section was hard to analyze because Pistol, who was the master of the shuffle, added to what Bennie played, and Uriel's steady beats really embellished what was already there.

How confused the outsiders must have been trying to figure out the drum sound. Most thought that it was only one drummer.

If you think that was confusing, the keyboard sound was misconstrued too. What was thought to be only Earl Van Dyke's full overwhelming piano sound was actually Earl *and* Johnny Griffith accompanying him. Sometimes Johnny would play the Hammond organ, and various keyboards. When we had multiple sessions these two guys would even trade instruments to give their fingers a break.

Joe Messina, Eddie Willis, and Robert White always held down the guitar section. If all three were not on a session, two would definitely be there.

How could three guitarists not get in each other's way and still be effective? The producer would have the arrangements prepared but the three would organize their parts and play them so flawlessly it would be like they were smoothly fused together. The aforementioned pieces of the rhythm section are what was referred to as the basics or foundation. Naturally there were other essential components that were a part of those sizzling tracks. You might say our contributions were comparable to a meal. The meats and breads are great, but the dessert complements the entire meal. And so with our music, it was the additional percussion instruments that made each production complete and gave it the Motown sound. We played vibes, congas, bongos, bells, blocks, tambourines, or anything that we could tap on to produce a musical sound. I was used a lot on vibes but most producers wanted me to play the tambourine because of the uniqueness of my style and sound. I was known to make any track come alive.

My style of playing is very distinguishable. If you listen closely, many of the Motown tracks mixed the tambourine track way up. My style of playing has been studied and practiced, but the uniqueness of my playing has proven to be too difficult to duplicate. Many musicians don't realize that I read music like a newspaper. On each tune I usually lock in with the drum lines.

Norman Whitfield was one of my greatest fans and according to him, I'm "the best that ever did it."

Listen for the dominance of the tambourine track on songs like 'War', 'Psychedelic Shack', 'Cloud Nine' and many of Norman's productions. Perhaps that will give you a clue to why I'm called Mr. Tambourine Man.

THE MARVIN GAYE TOUR

Marvin and the tour band rehearsed the show several times until he felt we were ready for the road. Our itinerary had been finalized and we were ready for our first stop – Alabama. We had been briefed on what and how to pack, as well as how to conduct ourselves in a place that previously had racial problems. We were traveling in a bus with limited space. On the bus were Marvin Gaye, Harvey Fuqua, The Spinners, Johnny Griffin (Marvin's assistant), five horn players, an organ player (Charles Harris), a drummer, conga player, bass player, guitar player and I played vibes and percussion. Including the driver there were about twenty-five people on the bus and one dog that belonged to Marvin. (Bow-Wow.)

This tour would be distinctively different for me. First, I wouldn't be riding in a hearse as I did when I worked back east. Secondly, the audiences would be much bigger, and Alabama had never been a part of my traveling experience. Alabama .. umm. Should we have any concerns for our safety? I had never visited the south, so naturally I had apprehensions because of the way African Americans had been treated in the past. I just wondered how we would be treated when we made our arrival there this time.

Since the gig was a one nighter, we had been instructed to wear something comfortable going down, but we would probably have to dress for the show on the bus a few miles before we actually got to the campus. We all met at Motown on the boulevard with our gear, instruments and luggage. For my own comfort, I took a pillow and a small blanket.

After a lot of getting on and off the bus, closing the cargo door, opening the cargo door, we were heading to the University of Alabama. I hardly slept or talked throughout the duration of the trip. Underneath, I was a little uneasy. I'm sure racial problems once existed just about everywhere, but my uneasiness probably resulted with the fact that I was from Philadelphia and hadn't been exposed to racial tensions. I visualized a huge sign posted on side of the road somewhere announcing the entrance of the deep south. Another thought was, when we crossed the Mason-Dixon Line, there would be a group of KKK members giving us the finger. I imagined all kinds of 'stuff'.

We rode for hours and hours making only a couple of stops for snacks and to relieve Marvin's dog. Well, none of the things that I had imagined about the south had happened yet. Geographically, the landforms had slightly changed and there were more trees and less concrete. The cotton fields and the corn fields rolled right out to the edge of the highway. The people in the south spoke a different language. Well, not really, but I couldn't understand the southern drawl or that deep southern dialect.

When we arrived at the university to do the gig for the students, they had gathered at the entrance gate waiting in anticipation. Marvin was popular from one side of the map to the other. Everybody loved his music and bought a lot of his records. Upon sight of the bus they began cheering and followed right behind the bus deep into the campus. All of the students were white. So I naturally became watchful of their every move. I wanted every member of the band to know, in spite of Marvin performing here, it was still 'Elvis Presley Country', and we were behind the cotton curtain. The bus driver (who incidentally was white) methodically parked in a space reserved just for our bus. It was right in front of a building marked OAZ Fraternity House. The Greek letters were different, but it was definitely a fraternity house. I thought the gig would have at least been in the gymnasium. We had dressed on the bus and were ready to go inside. A young man who seemed to be in charge directed us inside. We followed him down a narrow staircase consisting of about a dozen steps that emptied into a large basement room set up like a night club with tables and chairs. The capacity of the room was about two hundred. Before the show was over an additional one hundred stuffed the room. Students were sitting and standing everywhere, soaking up every inch of the room.

We set up our instruments and tuned up. Uriel Jones the drummer gave us the countdown, "1-2-1-2-3," and it was 'Show Time In Alabama, Ya-Hoo!!'

The Spinners were the opening act and they gave them an excellent performance with their synchronized moves and melodious voices. The compact size stage limited how much dancing they could do, but they managed. Most of the kids in the audience were all clad down in their western style costumes. They all carried guns in holsters that looked authentic. (This was not good.) It looked like we were filming a western movie. I played with one eye on the music sheet and one eye on the audience. The Spinners completed three tunes which had the audience ready to PARTY! The kids now had several drinks under their belts and were good and ready for the main crooner, Marvin Gaye, to 'get it on'.

They let that be known by chanting "We want Marvin! We want Marvin! We want Marvin!"

We didn't give them any opposition. "Bring on Marvin!" Bongo yelled to Marvin's assistant, Johnny Griffin. Now, Johnny always wanted to be noteworthy, and a part of the show. He would dress formally with a cummerbund, black trousers, white shirt, and bow-tie. We would joke with him about it and he would be heartbroken because we found him funny. We teased him for wanting to be more than just Marvin's assistant.

Marvin was about to hit the stage and Johnny reminded us to stand up when Marvin came on. (Standing up was Marvin's wife's suggestion.)

When the announcer shouted, "Here he is, Ladies and Gentlemen .. Marr-vinn Gaye!!!" the drummer and organist attempted to stand. Well, that went over like a fart in church. It was awful! You should have seen the fellows trying to stand and play at the same time.

Marvin hit the stage singing 'Hitch Hike'. The audience went absolutely, wild jumping and screaming loud enough to erupt your eardrums. The sounds were amplified because the place was so small. In spite of the cramped condition, some of the kids were trying to do the hitch hike dance, while the others continued to saturate their souls with Jack Daniels and beer.

Without showing any fear of inebriation, they guzzled the sauce like it was water. Their faces were red as beets and smoke was so thick you couldn't distinguish who the people were in the back.

After consuming a great amount of liquor, I knew the effects would become apparent and impossible to conceal. Like clockwork, they began twirling their toy pistols like they were on the ranch and were yelling, "Hee-Haw!" and "Yah-hoo!!." My gut feeling when I heard them yelling was things just might get a little out of control.

As the show continued, Don White (who was not white) had been making eye contact with one of the girls that crowded around the stage. I pleaded with him: "Look the other way, and forget any ideas you might have. Did you forget that we're in Alabama?"

The show was really rocking and Marvin was rapidly approaching the end of his repertoire of songs. The news spread in the audience like wildfire that "The band is ogling the girls." They didn't say just one band member but the whole band.

All hell broke loose. They started waving, and pointing their toy guns at us. Marvin sensed what was going on and concluded abruptly with a

My father, Roland Ashford

Uncle Base 1977

Me at ten years old

Me at fourteen

In the Army rifle team in 1958

The Carl Bell group. That is the first band that I ever played with. 1952 was the year. Carl Bell on drums and Jimmy Pringle on Organ, Rozzek on congas

Playing the vibes in 1963

Marvin Gaye sitting and Chico of The Spinners on tour in 1963

This picture was taken around 1976, soon after we arrived in Los Angeles in 1975. Left to right, Charlene, daughter Jakene, Jack and eldest daughter, Miko.

R: Johnny 'Hammond' Smith, Me, Leo Stephens and Eddie Mathias.

(Top) Me, Clarence Paul, Bob Cousar, Earl Van Dyke, Van Gordon Sauter (Bottom) Don Foster, Spider (Georgie Fame's drummer) and Booker Bradshaw

Beans Bowles (baritone
sax), Earl Van Dyke
and Me in 1965

L-R: Eli Fontaine
(saxophone), Earl Van
Dyke (B3 organ),
Robert White (guitar),
Bob Cousar (drums).

Earl and me in Britain in 1965

KIM WESTON
Tamla Recording Artist

With Bob Cousar and a
French musician

Monsieur Jack in Paris, 1965

From right to left: the tall guy with the 'Tam' is Jack, the guy standing is a French musician, and next to him is Stevie Wonder

big smile and: "Good Night everybody, I hope you enjoyed the show!" By that time Marvin was off the stage and probably in the room where he dressed. The atmosphere had become combustible and was ready to ignite. Someone in the audience yelled out, "Let's hang these niggers." We blazed the trail getting out of there with our instruments and jumped on the bus. There was only one way out, but it was a miracle that we made it without anyone getting hurt. Most of the students were blasted, and we were sober. Maybe that's how we got out so quickly. We put our instruments on the bus, the driver slammed the cargo door and we made a quick exit from the campus.

The loaded bus hugged the curvy road as we hastily made our way to the main highway. We were happy to be away from the liquor drinking cowboys, but a cloud of doubt lingered regarding our total safety until we were many miles north of the campus. The general consensus was that we barely escaped what could have been a calamitous ending. As the bus growled and gripped the highway, our spirituality and Christianity became quite evident as we praised and thanked God for our safety. That was the end of the southern gigs and no one complained.

We all rested much easier leaving the Mason-Dixon line behind us. We were both mentally and physically exhausted on the way back to Detroit but had enough energy to laugh about what had been an alarming situation that overwhelmed us with fear.

We arrived back in Detroit tired, sleepy, and in need of some serious hygiene. Harvey instructed us to go home and get some rest because we would be heading for the west coast soon on another tour. The rehearsals for this were scheduled back to back with long hours.

After two weeks we were ready to go again. Much of the same was done as the first tour. Our itinerary was approved, and Harvey briefed us on what to pack and how to act. The date to leave Detroit arrived and we boarded the bus for California. This time out it included Marvin, his wife Anna, Harvey Fuqua, and his wife Gwen, (please note that Anna and Gwen are Berry Gordy's sisters). Also on the trip were Hattie Littles, The Spinners, and the Marvin Gaye Band. The bus was filled almost to capacity. I felt good about the tour and knew it wouldn't be anything like the Alabama tour. It was late at night when we left Detroit and pretty soon everybody was asleep. The driver didn't waste any time getting to Oklahoma. This was our first stop at a motel. It was a long distance from Detroit and we welcomed the chance to get a shave, a bath and a good night's rest in a bed. After the stop we journeyed on to Window Rock,

New Mexico to an Indian reservation.

I think General Custer must have booked this show. I viewed the audience as the band and I set up our instruments on the stage. All I saw was Indians, Indians, and more Indians. Each one sat in total silence like they were at a funeral. The only movement was from someone being seated by an usher. The usual routine of the band was no different as the drummer gave us the countdown, "One-two-one-two-three." The first tune was an introductory tune because Marvin wasn't quite ready. We jammed hard and tried to arouse the Indians.

Picture this. At the end of the tune, no one applauded, no one smiled, nor moved one muscle. The placid faces just stared at us and remained motionless. Marvin was looking out from the wings and asked: "Damn, what am I supposed to do out there?"

I quickly remarked "Do anything, but don't tell any jokes."

Marvin hit the stage blasting with 'Hitch Hike' and on through his routine. After each of his tunes he got the same response, and he was jamming better than ever.

"Maybe one of you might have a special request," Marvin announced jokingly. Here again, no response. Even at the end of the show there was no applause. They just sat there.

Someone came on stage (an Indian) and announced that the show was over. I thought to myself, "What a dead audience." Really, I don't think they had ever heard of Marvin Gaye. Perhaps some tribal leader had booked us in order to steal their blankets while they were being entertained.

We did several other shows on reservations. Little did we know, the Indians loved the shows. They just were not in the habit of being demonstrative or emotional. If you didn't know, Native Americans are very warm and compassionate people. I'm glad because I don't think that I could have survived bows and arrows (smile).

We stopped at a few trading posts, mainly in New Mexico. Everybody was purchasing moccasins, turquoise, and other souvenirs. But me, I invested my 'green power' in a small handgun. There was no waiting period required for clearance and the gun was sold at a favorable price.

On our way to Phoenix, "a funny thing happened." I was actually expending energy in an attempt to get some rest. As I shifted from one position to another to avoid the loud sounds emanating from the rear of the bus, Marvin called out loudly, "Hey Jack Ashford, come back here." I was sleepy and really wanted to get some rest, but I hobbled to the back of the bus to see what he wanted anyway. "Come on man, get in this game," Marvin requested. In the game already was Chico, Pervis, Henry, Bobby, (The Spinners) Harvey Fuqua, Johnny Griffin, and of course Marvin. The space for actually gambling was quite restricted, barely allowing me to squeeze in. I watched for a few minutes as they shot the dice from between the seats and into the aisles. "Baby's gotta have a new pair of shoes," "Come on dice," and "Strike" were just a few of the phrases the guys were shouting, but it was clear that Chico was winning and he was also switching the dice. I didn't want to be the one to expose the cheating, so I just played a while and quit after I won about $400. I returned to my seat along with a couple other guys. I was about ready to make a second attempt to get a little rest when I suddenly heard Marvin shout, "Harvey! These so-and-sos have been cheating me. Chico's got three dice, and he's been switching the dice all along."

The strong displeasure in Marvin's voice could not have been matched even in hell at that moment. He was very, very angry. "Chico! I should make yo ass walk back to Detroit." They argued non stop for at least ten minutes. Marvin spoke so dramatically everyone riveted to his every word. No one could sleep through all of this turmoil and anguish. For the sake of peace and quiet, I was about to give him his money back when suddenly Marvin was calling my name.

"Jack Ashford!" He signaled the driver to pull over to the side of the highway. Now this is in the middle of the desert. Marvin yelled again: "Jack Ashford, get off the bus, 'cause I'm ga' whip yo ass. You knew they were cheatin' me and you didn't say nothing!"

I said "Remember you woke me up, and invited me to join your crap game. I never asked you anything about gambling. Plus, you were shooting dice a long time before you called me. So, how can you blame me for somebody else cheating you? Why don't you kick Chico's ass?"

I could see that he wasn't listening to me, so I just followed him off the bus. He was 'pissed to the highest peak of pistivity.'

Marvin had some boxing skills, but so did I. Boxing was one of Marvin's careers that he didn't pursue because he didn't want his face messed up. We sparred around for a few minutes and with my long reach, I had the advantage. My rationale motivated me to bring an end to the nonsense. I grabbed him and held his arms so that he couldn't throw any more punches.

"Marvin," I pleaded, "Let's stop this fighting. If I hit you in your 'chops' (mouth) this tour is all over, and everybody loses. His punches were not penetrating and Harvey could see that he was losing. Harvey quietly requested, "Y'all get back on the bus and sit down."

So Marvin just turned and got back on the bus, but not before he uttered one more threat. "Jack, as soon as we get to Phoenix, I'm ga' send yo ass back to Detroit."

I took in a couple of deep breaths and I too returned to the bus. All mouths were closed throughout the duration of the trip to Phoenix which was about two hundred miles. Anna and Gwen appeared to be disgusted and sat quietly too.

We arrived in Phoenix and everyone settled in for the evening. Some of us had had a 'rough day'. I showered and rushed to the bed for a few hours of sweet dreams. About the same time my head hit the pillow, I heard a knock on the door. It was Eddie 'Bongo' (the conga player). Eddie knew about the incident on the bus and explained to Marvin that I was innocent of his accusations. When Marvin heard Eddie's version of what happened, Marvin sent for me to come to his room. The first thing I thought about was that Marvin still had an axe to grind with me. I finally agreed to go after Eddie assured me that Marvin didn't have any malicious motives.

Eddie and I walked down to Marvin's room and found him smoking a joint. I almost got high just from breathing. There was a thick fog of smoke in the room. Marvin was sitting on the side of the bed as he invited us in. "Come on in man. I just want to talk to you. Bongo told me everything that happened on the bus and we're cool. No hard feelings OK?"

I warmly expressed my regrets and extended my hand out to shake his, and accidentally knocked over a whole shoe box of weed off the edge of the table on to the shag carpet, upside down. This was very serious! (even more serious than the bus incident). Marvin screamed: "Oh –! How in the hell am I going to get my weed out of the carpet? and don't say a damn word about a vacuum cleaner!"

I moved back slightly in case Marvin wanted to hit me. Bongo and I picked up as much as we could, but there was still some in the rug. When we left out of the room, Marvin was still trying to pick out the last of the seeds and fragments from the carpet. What luck! I had gone to Marvin's room to alleviate one problem and created another. He was OK though, and realized it was an unfortunate accident. I really felt bad.

We did a show in Phoenix and Marvin knocked the audience out again. He did his usual opener 'Hitch Hike'. The audience was mostly women and they went absolutely wild. The women wanted to take him home with them. They screamed and some seemed almost on the verge of fainting. His mere presence on the stage was enough for most whether he sung or not. They really loved him.

We were on the road again, with our next stop Hollywood. Soon after checking into the hotel, Marvin called a rehearsal. We were all set to rehearse but there was a problem.

Within just a few short hours, Pervis Jackson (one of the Spinners) had been arrested for carrying a weapon. This was an unregistered gun he had purchased in New Mexico, the same place I had bought mine. The rehearsal was cancelled and a few of the guys had to go and post bond to get him released from jail.

Even without the rehearsal the Hollywood show was remarkable. It would have been an excellent time to have recorded this live performance. The sound was complemented by the building's perfect acoustical structure. That's Hollywood for you. From Hollywood the show moved to San Francisco. The city hasn't been the same since. The place where we performed had standing room only and Marvin's performance was phenomenal. The deeper we got into the tour, the quality of his performance got better. I believe if he had been a candidate for Mayor, he would have had a landslide win in San Francisco. We did several shows there. One night, there was a very pretty young lady sitting on the front row. I tried desperately to catch her eye, but her attention was focused on another member of the band. When we returned to the hotel, guess who I saw? It was that same pretty girl that was at the show, dressed all provocative, and swaying her hips from the extremely east to west. She was a beauty. She walked right past my room, and spent the night with someone else. The next morning, the guy she spent the night with displayed a huge smile and was bragging about all the fun he had. We were a little envious at first. But as we were loading on the bus, a car pulled up that was marked 'San Francisco Health Department'. The health department official wanted to know, "Have any one of you had any sexual contact with a certain young lady?" You guessed it.... It was the same pretty young lady that had spent the night with one of the band members. The man had on rubber gloves and a hazardous material suit (not really, but this was our joke). "If you glow in the dark, man, you'll have to get off the bus." It was hilarious to everyone but the guilty party. The health official went on to say, "If any of you have had sexual contact with this young lady, I would advise that person to seek medical attention right away."

We just couldn't stop laughing. We packed the bus and moved farther up the coast to Portland, Oregon to finish the tour. We knew the music without looking at the charts and Marvin didn't miss a beat either. He wore his finest stage duds – a green suit with complementary accessories His hair was 'laid' with every strand in place. To put it mildly, he looked very dapper. This show was the best ever. The audience couldn't get enough and demanded an encore. Marvin didn't just do one encore, he did two. The crowd really got their money's worth. This was it for the west coast.

Instead of being in a hotel, this time we had small resort type cabins that had really thick plush towels that were fit for a king. Everybody commented how nice they were.

Marvin had personally gone to each cabin on the first day to remind us how to conduct ourselves – no loud noise, not to smoke weed, and most of all, "Don't take any of the towels." Everyone promised to act in accordance with his request.

When we were loading the bus for Vancouver, we had much more than we started out with, so it took extra time to maneuver the luggage and packages to make everything fit. Meantime, the manager of the motel came on to the bus and made a statement: "Someone has taken some of the towels from one of the cabins and we would like whoever did this to please give them back or we will have to charge this to your bill." Gee whiz, after all that pleading Marvin did, we couldn't believe that someone had taken the towels anyway. We began looking around the bus waiting for the culprit to confess. Nobody stood up and Marvin began 'raising hell'. "Why would you guys do something like this after me telling you not to?" he exclaimed with great disappointment.

I stood up and asked the manager, "What was the cabin number that had the missing property?"

The manager roared, "The cabin is number one."

All eyes turned to Marvin. Would you believe that was Marvin's cabin? His own wife had stuffed her expensive luggage with the towels and wash clothes from the cabin. Remember now, this is Berry Gordy's sister, who could afford to not only buy the towels, but was rich enough to buy the cabins and anything else. Needless to say, Marvin suffered total embarrassment behind that incident. So much for the 'Royal Family' and their 'Royal conduct'.

We journeyed on to Vancouver without any incidents and the show there went well too. The city was quite picturesque and we spent our spare time quietly seeing some of the sights. There was no drama and we did the gig without problems.

Three days later we arrived back in Detroit. My body was numb from the ride. The days behind me spent on the tour were so strenuous and tiring, I could only daydream about peaceful and tranquil hours under my own roof.

DETROIT! Once again I was home. I really welcomed the absence of the hustle, the bustle, the commotion, agitation and the turmoil.

Through it all, we had a million laughs. I enjoyed it all, but I was happy to be resting in my own bed.

THE FIRST MOTOWN EUROPEAN TOUR

I believe that any artist on Motown's roster would have relished the chance to be in Mary Wells' shoes during this golden age. It was 1963 and Mary Wells records were heard in every corner of the world. The Fats Domino-Little Richard era was long gone but had paved the way and left only traces of their success. As each Mary Wells record emerged from Hitsville, it was certain to be a chart buster. She was referred to by some as 'Motown's First Queen', not because she was the first artist to be recorded on the Motown label, but because she was extraordinary. She went on to sing a string of hits and her popularity swelled way beyond Berry's expectation.

Since Mary had performed at the Apollo, and had appeared on 'American Bandstand', I figured she had reached the pinnacle of her success. WRONG! As Mary's success heightened, it simply opened the door for her and other artists at Motown to become international touring artists. The phones were ringing off the hook. Europe was calling with great intensity. The Motown Sound had captured an audience mega-miles from Detroit, and they wanted desperately to nail down a tour. Instead of Mary Wells going over first, Kim Weston was booked for the first tour. This may have been done to 'feel out the market'. Remember, all of Motown's Revues were done in the United States, and thinking abroad was done with reservation. We heard the news, but couldn't believe what we were hearing. Many of the Motown tracks featured the vibes so, since I played the vibes, my name was down to accompany Kim.

England was named as our first stop. I questioned this fact. Was it really London, England or was it New England in the United States? I found it hard to believe that we would fly somewhere across the ocean rather than taking a bus to the gig.

It was not a mistake. We were definitely going to London. I immediately began thinking like a tourist....

I'll need five rolls of film, my camera, a light foldable raincoat, two pair of dark trousers, etc. I was excited and viewed this as a 'Safari of Pleasure' to see parts of the world that I hadn't seen yet. One of my favorite quotes was, "He who travels much, knows much." My friends chuckled when they learned of how I was packing and preparing for the tour.

The musicians that were going on the tour were called in for a briefing and given our usual 'how to act' tips. I had a few weeks before departure, and I definitely had plenty of time to repack and think 'musician' instead of 'tourist'. The touring band rehearsed the entire show with Mary and we were practically perfect. The rhythm was tight and solid. We had to be good because we were the first from Motown to tour abroad and this trip would set the tone for other acts in the future. Our goal was to return to the States with excellent reviews. Berry never engaged the entire studio band to tour. He always made sure that at least two or three were available to record when needed. On this tour Earl Van Dyke would be on piano and organ, Uriel Jones on drums, Robert White on guitar, and I played vibes and percussion. Kim Weston was traveling with her assistants.

We boarded the plane for New York, and just sort of blended in with the other passengers. No one knew who we were. I couldn't relax for thinking that we had to first go to New York instead of going directly to England. Once we landed in New York, we didn't have much time to waste before completing the preliminaries of getting our passports and ticket checks before actually boarding the plane. I was grateful for not being delayed. I was ready to trot the globe. The pilot moved expeditiously to the runway, and took to the airways as though he was anxious to get going also.

The trip went very well and without any problems. I napped a lot with an occasional walk to the rear of the plane. The service was absolutely great. We were traveling tourist, but received first class service.

When we arrived in London, we were warmly greeted by a group of wonderful people who were a part of the promotional crew. A very polished Englishman led the conversation with "Welcome to England! We are happy to have you but we have some bad news for you. The tour has been cancelled. We are very sorry."

That news was absolutely unexpected and unbelievable. We all needed face lifts. The cancellation had torn us apart. Earl said, "Do you mean that we have flown all the way over here for nothing?"

The promoter felt our pain and assured us that he would work hard to add us to one of his other tours with Gene Pitney, Bobby Shafto, The Kinks, Marianne Faithfull and Georgie Fame. These were all established European acts.

Several calls were made back to Berry about the dilemma we were in. We stayed nailed down to our hotel rooms until the deal was confirmed by the promoter. I had a chance to take in some of the sights, snap a few pictures, and soak up some of the European charm. The air was fresh and brisk, my kind of a tour. I figured that if the tour didn't happen, I would at least have some good shots. The word came down that the tour was a go and that made us all happy. The promoter provided us with an itinerary and the tour was set. The hour arrived when the bus pulled up draped with a big sign that read 'Kim Weston and the Motown Revue'.

As we burned the roads, people would notice us and respond differently. Some towns had never heard of Kim Weston and others knew exactly who she was.

They would applaud at the sight of the bus while others just stared. One thing that was common to all that attended the shows: the people called for repeat performances. We did gigs in London, Manchester, Leeds and a few other places, but the gig in Manchester was probably the best. It almost ended up in a tragedy, though.

The day after the gig, Georgie Fame invited me to ride back to London with him. I was bubbling with a bit of exuberance, so I readily agreed. Georgie was driving a fabulous brand new Jaguar sedan.

I knew this was a scenic highway so naturally I grabbed my camera to snap some more pictures. (The tourist/musician was well at work.) The drive going to London was without incident and we enjoyed exchanging some of our personal musical encounters.

Georgie couldn't hear enough about Motown. It was a great way to facilitate my favorite pastime, as well as bonding with Georgie.

Now, on the return trip to Manchester, it was a whole different story.

As we were coming down a mountain, Georgie lost control of the car and we slammed into a safety wall.

"Oh my God, did I come to England to die?" These were my first thoughts. It only took a few seconds but it seemed be an endless moment before the car came to a complete stop.

Whe-e-e-w. Georgie had the car under control and we were OK. Our hearts raced with fright and we were almost hyperventilating.

There were two sets of circumstances that helped us to avoid a bloody brush with death or even a fatal ending. First, the car was well crafted enabling it to withstand the serious impact, and secondly, the wall was so solid that it didn't give way to the crash. Shook up, and actually wondering if we were still alive, Georgie was able to pull over a short distance from the crash site. We got out of the car and took a look over the five foot wall. The drop down the mountain side was at least two hundred feet into a canyon. The condition of the car? Well .. the damage was mostly confined to the hood and fenders. It wasn't too bad considering our intact condition, but it was terrible for a new car to be all banged up. We drove on in to Manchester and counted our blessings. I've tried to expunge this harrowing incident from my memory but it never went into remission.

When I met up with the band again, did I have a story to tell? And, of course, (no mercy, no pity for you) Uriel Jones, who never passed up an opportunity to crack a joke said, "That's what you get for driving on the wrong side of the road. It happens like that every time." His humor brought about a big laugh from everybody.

The gig that night remedied my anxieties and did me a lot of good, Not only did Kim Weston and the band turn the place out, the British groups, like The Kinks, and Gene Pitney, brought the audience to their feet as well. We had never seen these acts on stage and became deeply enthralled in their performances. The magnitude of their talent beguiled us as though we were part of the paid audience. Man! They were sensational entertainers.

For three weeks the pace and routines were about the same. We would rest, travel, and do a show every night. As we traveled across England, I remember seeing some places (I believe out from Manchester) that still showed traces of damage from World War II. Some places hadn't even been rebuilt yet. We stayed in a hotel with the electrical system in great need of repair work. The place was like a big converted castle or an old mansion. It was massive in size and very cold. In order to engage the heating unit it was necessary to pull a cord and the heat would stay on for only fifteen minutes. When the fifteen minutes expired the heat would automatically go off, and the room would get ice cold – bone chilling cold. I would dash over to the cord for more heat and then dash back to cover up and try to get warm. By the time I got comfortable and warm, the heat would cut off and I was cold again.

I slept in a bed that was a hundred years old. It was a tall stately four-poster with a big fluffy mattress that seemed to have wrapped around me and I was slumped in the middle. I can't tell you how I felt sleeping in that old bed. I tried to envision which king or queen might have slept in this bed years ago. I didn't have any nightmares and didn't have any encounters with ghosts.

Before we left England we went shopping in the world famous Trafalgar Square. This place was a shopper's dream. Even if you didn't buy anything, the beauty of the place was worth every minute spent there. The giant waterfall captured everybody's interest. It was quite beautiful. It goes without saying I took pictures.

Earl had a habit of wanting everything that others had, and usually bought it. He fell in love with a pair of shoes that I bought and decided to buy a pair as well. I was aware that European sizes were smaller than American shoes, but Earl didn't know that. He tried on the shoes and knew they felt a little tight and assumed they would 'give a little'.

He liked the shoes so much he decided to wear them back to the hotel. After walking for a while his feet began to ache and throb. The thirteens he bought were really twelves, and he was almost tipping his feet hurt so badly. The 'Griz' was in agony. He walked backwards down a hill to take some of the pressure off his toes. This was a funny sight. We teased him continuously about the shoes all the way back to the States.

When we arrived back in Detroit, the work we had done in England was the talk of the company. The promoter had reported that the tour was a great success and the fans wanted another show from Motown. Our success served as a catalyst and laid the ground work for the next tour. We were the major players in the saga to come.

We had no time to rest much before we were back into the studio, overdubbing on the tracks recorded while we were on tour.

THE SECOND EUROPEAN TOUR

"Ladies and Gentlemen, we have a temporary hold up, but we will be departing shortly. Please bear with us." These were the assuring words from the airline stewardess. We were aboard a BOAC jet, bound for Europe .. precisely, England. We looked to each other and pondered. What could be causing the hold up? I thought for a moment that it could have been a statesman or some global dignitary.

The stewardess echoed the same message again. "Ladies and Gentlemen, we appreciate your patience for the hold up on take off, but we will be departing shortly." I had a window seat and I could see a couple of luggage handlers seemingly unloading some of the luggage from the cargo section. The compartment doors opened and closed several times. With a final slam of the cargo door, that assuring voice came on again. "Ladies and Gentlemen, thank you for your patience. We are now ready for take off." We all cheered and applauded to indicate our approval and thanks for ending the delay.

The plane had been held up by Berry Gordy and his private party. (He had that kind of power – to hold up the departure) He was displaying his multi-millionaire status. After boarding the plane, Berry couldn't find his camera. His assistant Don Foster had packed it in one of the bags that was in the cargo section of the plane. That's why the cargo door was being opened and closed several times. The luggage handlers had to search for the right piece of luggage and allow Don to remove the camera from the luggage and carry it on board. Berry sat in the first-class section and we were in the tourist section.

The plane was just a little over half full which allowed us plenty of room with a row of seats for each person. The pilot backed out and taxied down the runway. We were climbing through the atmosphere rapidly until we reached thirty thousand feet above the ground. Some were a little disturbed with the 'Houp-la-la' that delayed the scheduled take off, but Berry was having fun.

I didn't have a problem with Berry's power moves and definitely respected his success. We got along real good, almost as good as he and Smokey. I say 'almost' as good, because he never cut me in on any side deals as he did with Smokey. But, of course, Smokey earned his stripes with Berry. He had been with Berry almost from day one. I understood that and never tried to solicit any proposals to be his sidekick. I can't deny that I was slowly working on hammering out some independent success by dissecting what was involved in the process of making a hit record. I loved the Snake Pit, traveling, playing, etc., but I felt that it was just a rehearsal for my own projects.

The Motown aggregation consisted of Smokey Robinson, Ester Gordy, Earl Van Dyke, Eli Fontaine, The Temptations, The Supremes, Martha and The Vandellas, Ronnie White, Tony Newton, Robert White, Booker Bradshaw, Bob Cousar, Clarence Paul, Stevie Wonder, Beans Bowles, Van Gordon Sauter, Berry Gordy, and Don Foster.

This is the tour that 'Ready, Steady, Go!' was filmed on.

When the aircraft lifted from the ground in Detroit, the weather was great, and the sun was radiant and bright. There wasn't a cloud in the sky. As we moved across the map there were big mountains of white fluffy clouds in the distance, so beautiful they didn't seem real. They just bowed and acknowledged our passing with approval.

In no time we were over the Atlantic Ocean. This was a different story. Dark clouds were angrily dispatched from the heavens and bingo! We were in the midst of a frightful storm.

"Ladies and Gentlemen, this is the Captain speaking. We will be experiencing a little turbulence for a while, and you are advised to remain in your seats with your seat belts fastened. Please notice that the 'no smoking' sign has also been turned on."

This was serious, and everybody was concerned. "Ladies and Gentlemen, say your prayers, mother nature is sending an angry message without options," I uttered in an urgent tone to those near me. There was no shop talk, no laughter, no reading, nothing. We were totally silent. I was in prayer. I began quoting scriptures: "Out of the depths have I cried unto thee, O Lord."

The plane was dropping, and swaying all over the sky. At times you could hear someone cry out in fear: "Oh Lord!" "U-u-u-u!" and "Oh-h!"

The turbulence was tossing the plane around like it was a football. I buried my head deeper into my pillow and tugged on my blanket. Smokey was so uneasy, he drank and drank, but couldn't seem to get drunk. Of course Smokey wasn't the only one drinking. The tremendous 'light show' produced by the mile long vertical strikes of lightning, was too sensational for me to watch. The pilot repeated several times we would be in calmer skies soon, but 'soon' wasn't soon enough.

Eli said, "Man, we should have flown the friendly skies with United Airlines." We all became 'unglued', and managed to laugh..

We could feel the strength of the storm dissipating. The fire bolts of lightning had now been reduced to a flicker.

"Ladies and Gentlemen, this is the Captain speaking. The worst is behind us and we are less than a thousand miles of our destination, Heathrow Airport, England. Please notice that I have turned the seat belt sign off for now. We should be landing on time." How sweet it was to hear the pilot speak calmly and inform us we were a reasonable distance from England. The long hours in the sky, along with the mental stress, had both mentally and physically worn us out. We rested much easier for the duration of the flight. Everybody perked up when the stewardess instructed the passengers to 'prepare for landing'.

Hot Dog! We made it! I could hear the loud roaring engine's speed reduce as we circled the landing strip. The pilot slowly approached the runway and the tires squeaked after touching down. The plane reeled and rocked momentarily, until it was completely balanced on the runway. We taxied for what seemed to be half of forever. Everybody made an effort to jump up at once to gather their belongings from overhead and secure a place in the aisle. I just took a deep breath and gave thanks for making the trip to London safely. I grabbed my things from overhead and followed the others to the interior of the airport.

There were fans waiting everywhere. They were glad to see us and gave us a tremendously warm welcome, European style. It was the best! The fans had no reservations about letting everybody know that they loved and appreciated us. How exciting!

We were now breathing in England's air, walking on her soil, and visiting the home of Dracula, and Wolf Man. (I love horror flicks.) We were swept away on to buses, cabs and limousines to The President Hotel. This was a very prestigious four star establishment. Berry could really pick 'em. Signs of fall were splashed everywhere with beautiful browns, yellows, and oranges. The city was large, massed with people and had begun to show its age. The distant smoke stacks towered over the city bellowing out trails of gray smoke.

Like any other city, the deafening sounds of fire engines and police cars sometimes filled the air. Unless you appreciated the fine architecture of old stately buildings, you wouldn't have praise for the heavy columns and drab buildings. There were many sights to engage your camera for hours. If it wasn't a double-deck bus, or the changing of the guard, it was a castle or a cathedral. It was obvious that the English people were traditional and had conserved many of their aged landmarks. We hadn't checked in yet and I was already planning an adventure of sightseeing.

Upon arrival at the hotel, the lobby became instantly crammed with luggage and people. The normal everyday pace of guests along with the Motown aggregation and a sea of luggage made it seem like World War III had just been launched. Chaos was everywhere. The confused clerks tried to maintain their sanity as they assigned rooms and distributed keys.

After securing our rooms and getting our luggage put away, we all met for our usual 'how to act' meeting.

The hotel had provided a large conference room. Esther, like a mother, had gathered the 'family' together to point out some do's and don'ts of the trip, with the biggest – don't get into trouble in a foreign country. "Oh! And one other thing," she said jokingly, "always bow to the Queen."

Everybody scattered with their own little cliques and began exploring the nearby stores and shops. Checking in and the meeting with Esther had absorbed a lot of time and we hadn't eaten yet. My appetite was ravenous, and I could have eaten two of anything put before me. Two rhino knuckles, two mosquito legs – just anything to calm my appetite would have been sufficient.

Several of us rushed into what appeared to have been a nice place for a quick sandwich. Quick was nowhere to be found in the whole building. The service was awful. We waited at least for thirty minutes before we were given a menu. That was our cue to leave, but we thought that the service would get better. We ordered simple American-type sandwiches, and that took another thirty minutes. I took one bite and knew I was in the wrong place. It was like eating old gym socks put between two slices of bread, but at least it corralled the hunger until we had dinner. We didn't feel welcomed at all. I bet if the waitress knew we were Motown musicians things would have been a lot better. The next time, I'll wear my badge with my picture displayed on it. No tip for that waitress.

We anticipated jet lag, but felt good at the moment. After a quick tour of the immediate surroundings, we returned to the hotel for a brief rest before dinner. Upon entering my room, I found my roommate Eli Fontaine sprawled across the bed asleep, fully clothed and shoes off.

I think his feet were dead, because the odor reminded me of what I had smelled once at the funeral home. According to him he had a gland problem that affected his feet. (His feet?) I opened the door and asked him to please put his boots back on. In a voice that sounded like he had an accent he said, "OK, Mon." The air in the room improved slightly. It was a very slight change, because the smell circled the room and just lingered. For the duration of the trip, Eli kept his boots in his bag and wore regular shoes. He was a considerate and very nice guy. We had a lot of fun together and he was a very talented saxophone player. He is heard on the intro of Marvin Gaye's 'What's Going On'.

Dusty Springfield had made arrangements to cut a date with the rhythm section while we were in England. We relished the idea of cutting a date away from home. In addition to being excited, we welcomed a chance to pad our purse with a few extra bucks.

Esther Gordy made all of the arrangements before we left Detroit, and it was understood that we would be paid separately for the studio session. But Esther had an entirely different plan. The session went very well, and everybody was on a very 'high note' until we heard the news from Earl. He approached us with a troubled look on his face. We didn't know what was wrong, but we knew there was a problem.

"Well y'all, I know you expected to get paid right away for the Dusty Springfield session, but I was told by Esther that we will not get paid at all."

Our faces all looked blank and our lips were somewhat glued. After a moment or two, in a choral response, we all spoke together. "WHY NOT?"

Defensively, Earl explained, "It's not my idea of good business. I'm just the messenger, delivering the message." I didn't have much to say because I had seen some unfair situations before and this was just another one. My instincts were working and I felt that somehow we would get our money. We went to bed empty handed but rested up for the next place on the itinerary, Bournemouth. This town was in for one of the biggest R&B shows to ever be there.

With everyone shifting to overdrive, the long list of Motown performers would be churning out their hits, moving to the music and showing off their dazzling stage wardrobes. What a great show! These acts were not accompanied by English musicians picked up along the way, but by the same musicians that so brilliantly played on the original recording sessions. That was a very important element that enabled the acts to perfectly emulate their records.

Soon after our arrival we set up our instruments on the auditorium stage. Earl called us down from the stage for a short meeting. He cut straight to the point. "We're not playing tonight."

I didn't understand the reason, so I questioned him, "Why not? Why aren't we playing tonight?"

He looked at me and said, "Remember when we did the session with Dusty Springfield? We were supposed to have gotten paid for that as an extra gig. If they don't pay us our money right here tonight, then we ain't playing for this gig."

We all agreed. Actually, this was a call for a strike. The Supremes were close by and heard what we said. One of them informed Berry. The crowd was waiting for the show to begin and had grown a little impatient. Berry met with us backstage and wanted to know what was going on. Earl explained Esther's plan was unacceptable, and we would not play until we were paid. Earl went on to explain that the recording session had nothing to do with the tour, and furthermore Dusty's company had paid Esther for the date. Nobody could believe she would ever consider thinking of this 'below the belt' behavior. After hearing and digesting what Earl had said, Berry sort of rubbed his head and assured us that we would be paid immediately after this gig.

"Just go on out there and play. I guarantee you'll be paid right after tonight's show." We felt that Berry was a man of his word and returned to the stage. After the countdown, we played our hearts out like nothing had ever happened. That night The Supremes opened and 'turned the place out'.

Hundreds had piled into the auditorium and were overwhelmed with these dazzling megastars. They were gleaming in their sequined gowns, shiny shoes and bouffant wigs. When those ladies finished their list of songs the audience cheered, jumped, clapped, screamed, and one other thing ... they threw little hard things that were wrapped like candy on to the stage.

Much to my surprise, it was candy. We were a little perplexed at first because no one had warned us about the English custom of throwing candy. If the audience really liked the performance they would shower the performers with candy. We thought at first they were angry and intended to hurt us. The candy was collected by an attendant and resold for the next show.

Just like synchronized clockwork, Martha and the Vandellas, Smokey and the Miracles, Stevie Wonder, and finally The Temptations, graced the stage and the showers of candy followed each performance. The audience was very pleased.

The tour moved further north and at each of the stops the welcome mat was laid out for us. We performed to sell-out crowds and the acts were mobbed for autographs and pictures. Some of the fans just wanted a glimpse or to just touch one of the performers.

The fans were great and really appreciated what they had heard and seen.

We had been traveling now for about five days in cities north of London. The large bus windows afforded me a panoramic view of the quiet serenity that the rolling hills and mountains offered. I became lost and engulfed in the magnificent countryside that innocently stood guard over its valleys. My concentration was broken as my eyes converged upon some strange looking big mounds of something white resembling melons, stacked in a field.

I couldn't figure it out. I said to the bus driver, "What are those big stacks of white things out in the field?"

He explained, "They are stacks of turnips."

I asked, "Where are the green tops?"

He quickly had an answer for me. "Oh! They give those to the hogs."

I couldn't believe what he was telling me. "Man, if you tried to give greens to the hogs in the States I'm afraid you'd get hurt. People in the US love greens and would never feed the green tops to their animals. That's the best part."

We had performed in Birmingham, Coventry, Leicester, and Sheffield. Manchester was about the halfway mark of this European tour, and was our next stop. On the way there everybody was very hungry. The trouble with that was there were no restaurants open late at night, so we had to roll on. We kept our eyes stretched for an open place that served food. The bus sped down the highway and we kept looking, but everything was closed.

About daybreak, just inside Manchester, the driver pulled into a small, seedy Bates Motel-looking place.

The food (what little they had) was displayed buffet style and had been wiped out by the first eight or ten in line. There were at least thirty more hungry mouths who were ready to riot for food. We were starving.

The little, almost midget-sized cook/waiter took a look at all of the African Americans lined up and sputtered the words, "I-I-I-d-on't have any more food. I didn't have any idea that you were coming."

Melvin spoke with his deepest baritone voice that sounded like the voice of the Jolly Green Giant: "What do you mean you don't have any more food? Find some; we're hungry!"

With frustration written all over his face, he paced back and forth in an effort to think of a solution.

Someone shouted out "What about this little blind boy, Stevie? Don't you have something for him?"

The answer came from someone in the line. "F--- the little blind boy."

The lucky ones stood in line to pay. I'm sure that we probably overpaid the restaurant owner because we couldn't count British money. We just handed him some bills. The sandwich I had was wrapped in waxed paper.

I headed for the bus to sit and finally enjoy what I bought. I made the discovery that I had two pieces of almost raw bacon between two slices of bread. I swore that I couldn't eat it and someone came from behind me and took it right out of my hand.

We drove deeper into Manchester. There we were properly fed.

As the bus moved along we would all sing and clap our hands. The bus driver would bob his head with enjoyment. He was well entertained.

Diana had continuously bitched about the conditions on the bus. It was too cold, too crowded, seats too hard and just no place for a diva. We had shared the same bus seat almost for the whole duration of the trip. The bus wasn't the greatest and she had been complaining to Berry to do something. I gave her most of the blanket and let her sit close to the heat duct. That wasn't really enough, so after we ate, Berry arranged for a limo to transport him and The Supremes to the next stop.

Well, of course, Martha Reeves absolutely raised the roof off the bus. She thought that it was terrible to leave them on the bus and allow The Supremes the luxury of a limo. The fellows teased me by saying that Berry didn't care about Diana being cold, he wanted to make sure that I wasn't trying to 'warm her up', since we shared the same seat and same blanket. They asked me if I could walk on water, because Berry was going to make me walk back to Detroit.

After the complaints, Berry's assistant engaged another bus that was in better condition and we were more comfortable. In spite of the cold bus I would say that the Manchester food situation was the worst part of the trip.

The remaining shows on our itinerary were in Leeds, Newcastle, and then across the border to Scotland. All of these shows went well and without a hitch. Our transportation was good, the food was good and no one had any problems. Well, maybe one – the weather.

When we arrived in Scotland we had a day off, but the skies were dark and the overcast encouraged us to stay in the hotel. Everybody had their own suites and in each one something would be going on.

In the Temptations' suite, we were listening to music and a lot of pot smoking was taking place. All you had to do was walk in and inhale. Bam! You were high. They told me to go to the lobby and read the paper or find Sherlock because I didn't get high and I was off limits.

With my black-rimmed 'Clark Kent' glasses, white socks and wool buttoned sweater, I appeared to be the nerd of the entire group. Martha Reeves was there along with the Vandellas, Stevie Wonder, two of the Supremes, Clarence Paul, a few musicians, and some of the assistants.

Everybody wasn't smoking, but everybody was having a good time playing cards, dancing and drinking. It was our own private party. No one was boisterous. In spite of the high spirited activities everyone acted with total regard for the next door neighbors. But then a loud knock was heard. It was so loud, it sounded like the police. Everybody looked to one another wondering who could it be. Anyone that wasn't in the room knew to call first.

BAM! BAM! BAM! The knock came again. Someone opened a window, and someone else started fanning the thick clouds of smoke. "OK guys I don't want to use force to gain entry to this suite and I would suggest that you open this door NOW!" Thank goodness the voice was familiar. Someone peeped out to make sure who it was, opened the door and in steps Berry. He made a couple of steps inside, slammed the door, and looked around to make eye contact with each individual. Everyone reacted as though their own father had walked in. Some offered lame excuses like "I just came down to borrow a record," or "I was just leaving."

The truth was, they were embarrassed that Berry had walked in on the party where people were smoking pot.

"I want everyone to have a good time, but you have been warned to stay out of trouble while you are in a foreign country," Berry insisted.

He looked at me and said, "You don't look like you belong in here, come on and go with me." He knew that I didn't smoke or drink. We went to his suite that was located on the other side of the hotel. Berry knocked on the door and Don Foster let us in.

My relationship with Berry was always friendly and respectful. I never saw his negative side some of the others complained about. "Come on in, Jack, do you remember our dice game we use to play?"

I declared, "Do I? Man-n-n I used to beat you unmercifully." It was no surprise, when he had a few exchanged words for me.

"Well now, do you think that you can do it again?"

With certainty in my voice, I quickly responded, "Bring on the dice."

We had our own little friendly game of dice whereby we would each take a pair of dice, throw them against a wall of some kind, and the one with the highest numbers would be the winner .Don became the score-keeper of the 'Beat My Number Game', but I also kept score in my head to make sure that he wasn't cheating for the boss. He won that particular game, but I had beat him plenty before this. I teased him and told him I had let him win.

"Well, do you want to try to 'let' me win again?" Berry jokingly asked. We laughed it off and I retired to my own room.

I remembered an incident when we were playing in a theater back in England, another instance of me and Berry competing. We were admiring the beautiful ladies that had come to see the show. There was one in particular I told Berry that I was going to get. She put a twinkle in Berry's eyes too. So he made me a bet that he could get her and I wouldn't.

Berry was a true gentleman and warrior and never mentioned to her that he was the world-known Berry Gordy, the owner of Motown Records. He just used his charismatic charm and efforts that didn't seem to work good enough to get the girl that day.

By the way I got the girl.

Stevie was frequently pampered by somebody all of the time. He was like our little brother or the 'baby'. Despite his encumbrance, Stevie was truly a 'wonder' in every sense. He could sing, play several instruments, and when in the studio, could move around in it better than some of those with 20-20.

There was one major problem. Stevie had 'BADDDD' hair. It was very difficult to manage. On one of our 'down time days', Clarence Paul (who usually cared for Stevie) had to make sure that Stevie's hair was looking good for the next show. Ordinarily, this would pose no problem but Stevie's extraordinary bad grade of hair required extra effort and exertion. Each strand gripped his head extremely tight. Clarence had brought along a jar of Jabra super strength hair straightener.

He completed the preliminaries by applying Vaseline around Stevie's face, neck and ears in order to avoid burns from the strong solution.

Clarence tried combing Stevie's hair first and broke a tooth out of the comb. He continued by applying the white cream that resembled lard with a large tooth comb to Stevie's hair. All of this took place in the bathroom. When Clarence had finished applying the Jabra, he told Stevie, "Just sit here and when your head starts to burn, let me know."

The music was jamming and Stevie was bobbing his head and clapping his hands when suddenly he called out "Clarence, Clarence, it's burning!"

However, Clarence didn't hear him. So Stevie started jumping up and down violently this time screaming "Clarence! Clarence! Clarence!"

I yelled to Clarence, "Stevie's hair is smoking" He came over and Stevie was dancing as though someone had put a torch to his butt. So Clarence rinsed his head and relieved the burning. The straightener had his hair looking like a herd of cows had been licking on his head. Clarence was able to comb his hair out. Within minutes Stevie's hair took on a life of its own and started curling up like coil springs. Clarence became quite perplexed because he had never seen Jabra fail, and there was nothing more he could do.

Clarence styled Stevie's hair and was able to make his 'process' look good. He put Stevie's 'Do Rag' on and told him to relax and enjoy the music. Of course, we all found it quite hilarious and couldn't stop laughing.

The last show was in a Scotland auditorium. The newspapers had spread the word that the Motown Revue was sensational and we felt it was our task to live up to their expectations. The musicians had a special rehearsal to make sure we made the proper adjustments with the music. We wanted this 'swan song' to be a night to be remembered.

The show went just as we had envisioned. Martha and the Vandellas, Stevie Wonder, The Supremes and The Temptations were supremely good. This was truly a command performance by each act. The audience got an earful and they demanded a repetition. "ENCORE! ENCORE! ENCORE!" They shouted over and over again. The band began playing and all of the acts returned to the stage with a grand finale.

By now the crowd had started gathering closer and closer as though they wanted to come on to the stage with the performers. The ushers and guards kept the crowd back as the last song was completed. Some of the crowd waited outside to get autographs and pictures of the stars. We had to literally wade through a sea of fans to reach our bus.

The tour was now over and the reviews were all astounding. A+, A+, and A+ again.

Berry was very pleased with the entire tour and commended us on the professionalism, the sophistication and style exemplified away from home. The audiences in that great country had been the best, which brought out the best in us.

We had closed at the Olympia and everybody was on a special high (without drugs). We felt especially good because the tour had gone so well and we had been totally accepted by all of the European audiences. Our bags were packed and visions of Detroit danced in our heads. We were anxious to share our experiences with those back home, as well as a few gifts and souvenirs. We crowded into buses, taxi cabs, and limos and headed on out to the airport to BOAC Airlines ticket counter.

We were allowed a certain amount of luggage, which none of us had a problem with. But there was one problem. We had exceeded our limit because of the extras the little blind boy, Stevie had purchased. He had bought an amplifier and a keyboard. We all had to chip in and pay for the extra weight which we really didn't want to do, but we wanted to return home.

We had some time left before our departure and decided to get something to eat in the airport diner, (Stevie too). We talked and laughed and had a nice snack. Earl whispered and said to pass the word "Let's leave Stevie's little ass sitting in here alone and make him pay the bill."

The word spread quickly, like wildfire, and one by one we eased out and left Stevie talking to himself, and rocking his head back and forth like a cobra with shades on. He realized that he was alone and he ended up paying the food bill. He was steaming with anger and thought that was a dirty trick.

When we returned home we had a lot of stories and pictures to share with the Motown family that didn't go. As soon as we got a little rest it was business as usual.

We were called to lay down the tracks for some more hits.

THE MIKE TERRY CONNECTION AND JUST PRODUCTIONS

Just being able to say that I knew Mike Terry is awesome. He was a very skillful musician, writer, and saxophone player. He became known for his signature performances on 'Baby Love', and all of the early Motown sessions of the sixties. You could easily recognize his playing because it would just 'reach out and grab you'.

His style was very distinctive, and imitated by others. People would always ask "who is the sax player?" Man, he would growl through the tracks as no other could.

Mike and I sort of gravitated toward each other because we wanted to achieve the same goals. Our conversations were usually about growing in the record industry and 'cashing in' on our talents.

We didn't see much opportunity for advancing at Motown. We had grown weary of Motown's insensitivity toward our individual creative development and advancement. The Snake Pit was constantly in use by producers whose activities reminded me of ants attacking a sugar pile. Our chances of penetrating the existing line up of writers and producers, appeared to be slim and none.

After a session one day we sat on the Motown porch and talked. As usual we discussed our growth and what we were going to do about it.

"Jack, why don't we get together and write some songs and develop some material on our own?".

Without stammering, I quickly responded, "That's exactly what I want to do! We owe it to ourselves to develop and become more than just studio musicians."

Mike and I agreed that since Hank Cosby and Mickey Stevenson had a firm lock on 'opportunities' we had to go for it. Mickey's nickname was 'Il Duce' – the nickname for Mussolini – which was very fitting. Hank was a saxophone player on some of the sessions. When he wasn't doing that, he wrote some charts as an arranger and was involved in various production ventures.

With so many dependable producers in place at Motown, the competition was inevitably tough and it could make it hard for songwriters to get their songs produced.

Take this as an example: Eddie Willis, guitarist and a Funk Brother wrote the song 'Home Cooking'. When Junior Walker's recording of the song was released, he found the author credits a little 'strange'. This happened in 1966. All of this is not to trash anyone, it's just the raw facts.

In 1966 Mike and I started spending a lot of our spare time writing songs together. I lived in the Palmetto Apartments, at 110 John R. Street. It goes without saying the apartment was not conducive for playing instruments and writing songs, so I would drive to Mike's house.

My knowledge of producing was limited. I had a lot of ideas bottled up inside my mind, but needed a little direction on how to best present them.

Mike knew more about producing than I did and taught me a lot. He had a lot of patience and was a tremendous teacher. His teaching technique was unique because he would be teaching you and you wouldn't realize you were learning. I had written songs before, as well as attempting to make them sound commercial with my arrangements, so I wasn't totally green to what Mike was trying to teach me. Our collection of songs was growing in number and we had created some pretty impressive stuff.

We had used a few people as critics who strongly encouraged us to somehow get our productions heard and released. By now, the news of our intentions had journeyed back to Motown and we were not called to do any sessions. We didn't have to worry about turning in any resignations – we were not fortunate enough to have a contract or guaranteed salary.

Golden World Recording Studios was owned and operated by Ed Wingate. Earl Van Dyke had been cutting sessions for Wingate and made arrangements with him for me and Mike to do the same. One of the first tunes I played on at Golden World was 'Double O Soul' released on Edwin Starr.

Mike and I started lending our talents to producers and writers that were already on staff with Wingate. Soon after we were also put on salary and our first project was to produce a song in the San Remo Strings Album called 'Lonely Man', (or maybe 'Lonely One'). Gil Askey did the string arrangements and Mike and I did the rhythm arrangements.

Our tenure at Golden World was less than a year. This was the experience we needed to validate our capabilities.

Our next move was probably spiritually driven. We opened our own company. The building was located on the corner of Livernois and Joy

Road, with the unforgettable name of Pied Piper Productions. Shelly Hanes was the third partner. He had worked with Mike and me at Golden World. He recognized our talents and joined forces with us. Shelly was generally resourceful in acquiring production opportunities. Once he read in *Billboard* that a James Bond movie needed a sound track. We did in fact create a tailor-made Bond production of 'You Only Live Twice', but of course, we didn't have Paul McCartney to sing it. Instead, Lorraine Chandler was the artist. James Bond logos were all through out the track and I'm still proud of our workmanship. And hope one day to release the tune.

Pied Piper was like the forerunner to Just Productions, which opened the door for arrangers like Joe Hunter, Dale Warren, and others that I kept busy. I produced a lot of recordings and these guys arranged and played.

Pied Piper was somewhat of a 'spin-off' of Golden World. Our first artists were Lorraine Chandler and Mickey Farrow. I was introduced to Lorraine by a drummer, George McGregor. She had dropped out of college after the death of her mother to assist with the rearing of her younger siblings. She had aspirations of becoming a Motown artist, especially since she was a friend of Otis Williams, a member of the Temptations. Of course, being a native of Detroit, she knew a few others that were also employed there.

We talked to Lorraine about the advantages of being a part of Pied Piper which mainly was she would be our prime project. She came in and let us hear her voice so that we could match her voice to one of the songs we had already written or write a new one for her.

Lorraine didn't really knock us out as a singer, but she had an impressive way of attacking the tracks with a lot of energy. There were certain inflections in her voice that gave her delivery a quality that was worth pursuing.

We had just the song for her, 'What Can I Do?' She learned easily and had the burning desire to become a star. Lorraine had a powerful voice and projected her agressiveness on tape. She sang with feeling and the sound of her voice on tape was excellent.

With the Funks on the rhythm tracks the production was 'solid'.

I thought out loud, "Mike, we're on our way with this one." A big burst of laughter from Mike let me know that he felt the same way. We released the song on the Giant label and the publishing company was Earlbarb. (The name Earlbarb was derived from Mike's wife's name

Barbara and my lady's name Earlene).

One of RCA's promotion men heard 'What Can I Do' on the radio and before long, some of the deal makers from RCA were contacting us. They made it clear that they really wanted that record. It was a done deal for Mike, Shelly and me. Lorraine was now an RCA artist and we were ready to cut other acts that we had on our roster.

We had the Cavaliers, The Metros, The Hesitations, Freddie Butler, Nancy Wilcox, Willie Kendrick, and Sharon Scott.

Sharon was a cute and sweet young lady that everybody admired. She was a sensational singer, whose physical make-up perfectly matched her voice. I felt somewhat akin to her because she was a native of Pennsylvania which is the same part of the country where I'm from. I can't remember who introduced me to her but it was great. We had the perfect song for Sharon which was 'I'm Putting My Heart Under Lock And Key'. Both releases generated a lot of popularity. RCA now wanted as many releases as we could crank out.

The demands were almost insurmountable. The more we produced, RCA demanded more and more.

We had a decent budget to record with and we cut songs on just about everybody, including Mickey Farrow. The production on her, like the other releases, were popular in Europe, but it was extremely hard to get a record played in Detroit.

KAPP Records was another company that was made available to us through Garrard Percell.

The deals were really coming in and we were kept very busy trying to fulfill our obligations. Paul Robinson was one of the A&R men at RCA that authorized Percell's record deals. We didn't own a studio, but United Sounds certainly loved us. There were a few other studios that we used but 95 per cent of our recording was done at United Sounds.

The relationship between Mike and I as writers and producers, was interrupted by the behavior of Percell toward Shelly. Working conditions became stressful and unpleasant.

Beyond that, we were overloaded with volume and not given adequate time for developing artists. We were swindled out of a couple of artists because of the way the deals were constructed on paper.

Mike and I called it 'quits' as partners, but we remained friends. For a moment we had to 'regroup and refocus'.

Lorraine went with me along with Eddie Parker, Billy Sha-rae, Al Gardner, and Sharon Scott. Mike went to Chicago to do some productions with Josie Armstead, and Mickey joined him.

My bank roll was fairly decent and I continued cutting at a furious pace. I then became associated with Hugo & Luigi, and cut a few tunes on Luther Vandross for this team.

With Mike gone from the company, I used Paul Riser to do the arrangements. It was the dawning of a new day and I was about to embark upon a new 'undertaking'.

The building at 6099 Whitewood became the headquarters for Ashford Records and Just Productions. I rented the second floor, while another tenant occupied the first floor.

Likely my loud music disturbed them because they soon moved. The building's owner was a man that I met at Golden World Studios. He was Joanne Bratton's step-father. When the downstairs became vacant I rented both up and downstairs. We now had a good 800 square feet of space to live and work in. We converted the downstairs kitchen into a studio. That required installing soundproofing and burlap. (You'll be surprised at how R-30 insulation works for soundproofing.)

I had a couple of guys that assisted with the soundproofing: Jimmy Coleman, a songwriter and a faithful friend, along with George Rountree, a keyboard player, did a superior job. We covered the windows with soundproofing also. In fact the job was done so professionally, I never received one single complaint about noise.

We had worked like little beavers getting everything ready. In the studio I had a Spinette, a reel to reel tape recorder, a four track, and a mixer. We had turned a white woodframed house into a recording studio and administrative office, where we could do our demos.

Need is the mother of invention, and I learned a lot independently about engineering because I had to. I would mix and do a lot of creative things in preparation for a studio session. Everything was tried and tested before engaging musicians at the studio. I learned that lesson from Mike when we were partners.

I cut a lot of sessions at United Sounds, Richard Becker's Pac Three, and at Danny Dallas' Studio. The Pac Three Studio was a converted garage that had a wonderful sound. Many of the producers around town were reluctant about recording there, but I was always happy with the quality.

I was instrumental in getting Tony Camilla, Brad Shapiro and Dave Crawford to record there. Dave Crawford recorded Wilson Pickett, Candi Staton, and a popular gospel singer, Dorothy Norwood. They all loved it at Pac Three. This was a true test having the heavy hitters to use the facility.

This was around 1972. Make no mistake, I was tremendously confident in my productions and wasn't afraid to be a little bit more creative and experiment with different sounds. Take the 808 kick drum that's now used in rap music. I was utilizing that sound back in the early seventies. That sound was like a big parade drum with a big BOOM-BOOM sound that would rock you.

Something else, I double tracked lead voices when some of the other guys wouldn't. Believe me, I wasn't lacking in the department of creativity.

By me 'divorcing' Motown temporarily, it allowed me to have the opportunity to expand my creativity, and become an even better musician. So really Berry was the recipient of that hiatus that I took.

Lorraine had developed her skills beyond singing long ago and was now competent in other areas of the business. Like a common expression we use around the 'shop', she could 'hear'. This means she could easily determine if a musician played incorrectly, or if a vocalist sung incorrectly. Much of this was developed from her singing background. She actually had to learn how to blend her voice without 'out singing' everybody else. She had a lot of ability that was just waiting to surface.

After combining what Mike and I had taught her with her own abilities, she was a very capable producer, and played a major role in the company. Lorraine was devoted to the success of the company and worked long hours in the office to complete copyrights, writers agreements, and other necessary documents.

When we became pressed for money, she didn't hesitate to get a job to help the company stay afloat.

In addition to the artists we had at Pied Piper we now had The Smith Brothers and Saundra Richardson. (Saundra's voice was almost identical to Gladys Knight's.)

Occasionally a production deal would make its way to Just Productions. Bobby Martin, (whom I had known and been friends with since back in the fifties) had approached us about producing Don Gardner and Baby Washington. We did in fact produce them, but I never found out if the tunes were ever released or not.

They were great songs with James Jamerson doing a stellar performance on the tracks. This was just one more time that James demonstrated his unquestionable versatility of playing any music other than the music created by the producers at Motown. We had trouble doing our job, listening to the genius work his magic with his bass guitar.

Each day of work at Just Productions always represented another day closer to our dream. Our artists would drop by sometimes unannounced because we had an open door policy. They would collaborate on songs with other writers and artists.

Our roster looked real good in terms of talent. What Billy Sha-rae lacked in vocal skills and ability, he made up for with energy and a great band. He was a good looking guy and always performed to a packed house. When I would listen to his performances on 'I'm Gone', 'Do It', and even 'Let's Do It Again', I could feel energy pulsating through the entire room.

Those were good records and are still getting European play thirty years later. We released four tunes on him.

While it's true that Billy was a heartbreaker and a handsome guy that the ladies all loved to fantasize about, my dog hated him. 'Baku' (my dog) would show resentment for Billy more than anyone else that would ever visit me. He just couldn't tolerate Billy Sha-rae. Baku was somewhat of a passive Doberman until Billy came around. He wanted to tear his head off.

Now, Al Gardner was a tremendous singer who was very emotional with every song. He made you really feel what the lyrics were saying. If it was a 'I can't live without you baby' song he was singing, he made it seem like there was really someone out there that he couldn't live without. 'I Can't Stand It' was his best release.

Eddie Parker lived in Saginaw, Michigan, but would come down to Detroit and cut sessions every week. Eddie could scream like Otis Redding and Wilson Pickett combined. His soulful delivery was quite commercial. He was a diabolical soul singer. From the day of his audition with Just Productions until his last, he never ceased to amaze me with his strong will and determination to find his niche in the world of R&B. We released four songs on him and those were also big sellers in Europe.

Saundra Richardson was another extraordinary talent that did everything right, but was doomed because of her 'Gladys' sounding voice. We cut some real electrifying songs on her but no matter who heard them, the response was often the same: "She can really sing, but she sounds so much like Gladys Knight."

The competition was serious, but she was not intimidated and connected with producer/arranger Tony Camilla in hopes of getting a tune hot enough to climb the charts to a respectable position. Tony cut a real nice song on Saundra called 'I feel a song in my heart again', but it was taken from her and given to Gladys Knight. That was a real heart breaker.

I want to deviate momentarily and tell you a little about Tony Camilla. He was a little Italian guy about five-foot-five that constantly bragged about his cooking – Italian cooking that is.

I was very much into Lorraine's collard greens and ham hocks and couldn't imagine anything happening in my kitchen Italian.

"Jack, you can't let me leave Detroit without making everybody an Italian dinner, please, OK?" pleaded Tony.

"Can you cook?" I asked. "Tell me, did you bring all the stuff you need in your luggage? 'Cause we don't have anything in the cupboard that even resembles Italian."

"I will have to go to the supermarket to pick up a few things, but I guarantee, you will enjoy what I'm going to make," Tony said with confidence.

"OK, but you know you'll never live this down if you fail."

Lorraine took Tony to the supermarket and bought everything needed for this Italian feast. When I say everything, I do mean everything. He bought olive oil, hamburger, Italian bread, wine, garlic, oregano, onions, tomato sauces and bags and bags of everything Italian. The only thing missing was Frank Nittie and Al Capone. He generously seasoned the food with wine and poured a glass or two to sip on while he was cooking. Richard Becker observed more than cooking going on in the kitchen and demanded, "Tony, Give me that wine bottle!" He took the bottle of wine and gulped it down.

With Richard being of German descent, he should have been able to control his liquor a little better. In no time, his eyes began dancing around in his head, his speech became slurred and he actually staggered. Tony had turned tomato red and he was feeling his liquor too. This was hilarious to Lorraine and me because we didn't drink.

"I need more pans!" Tony yelled out.

"All we have is what you see. Are you sure you need more than seven?" I asked. Pots and pans were everywhere and it looked like Tony had been cooking for an army. The kitchen aroma had attacked my senses and my taste buds were anxiously awaiting that delectable meal.

The table was perfectly set, and Chef Camilla finally invited us to sit down . "What a spread! This is unbelievable – Mamma Mia!" I had to just look at the food for several minutes. I only recognized the spaghetti, but I was willing to trust the mouth watering aroma to devour everything in sight. Tony had become the cook of the century and believe me, the food was exquisite and we 'ate our lights out'.

Lorraine and I really had some notable singers on our roster. Telma Hopkins and Joyce Vincent (who went on to sing with Tony Orlando) were once the background singers for the company. Telma also became an actress, and appeared on a couple of TV sitcoms.

She has experienced great success. Thelma and Joyce are the background voices that are on Sharon Scott's record, Lorraine Chandler's record, and a few others. Telma's voice was as clear as a bell. I remember once the Funk Brothers had a date to accompany Diana and the Supremes but Diana was unable to work. Telma replaced Diana that night and sang all of the lead parts and, I might add, she did an outstanding job.

I consider Pied Piper to have been a good breeding ground for what we wanted to do in producing a volume of productions.

HOLLAND-DOZIER-HOLLAND

Berry Gordy's 'Dream Team', Holland-Dozier-Holland, was the greatest team of writers to ever penetrate the Motown walls. Decades have passed and they still hold an unimpeachable position for their brilliant accomplishments as masters of lyrics, melodies and productions. Song after song, hit after hit, they kept the charts smoking. It was as though they controlled the reins of professional attainment that guided their talents beyond their own imagination. HDH was (without any controversy) the hottest writing and production team in the record industry. The number one spot on Billboard's charts seemingly was reserved for this awesome threesome's powerhouse of tunes. 'Bernadette', 'Where Did Our Love Go?', 'Baby Love', 'Stop! In The Name of Love' – and that's just to name a few of the hits the HDH team authored.

Eddie Holland and Brian Holland did most of the lyrics while Lamont Dozier played the chords for the tracks. Their relationship was like a match made in heaven.

Just as the moon progresses through its successive phases, HDH felt their time with Motown had gone through its phases and had 'phased out'.

In 1968, HDH had become discontented and had a lengthy list of unsolvable problems. Brian, who had been a part of the nucleus of the company, gathered up all of his marbles and ran with his crew to launch a new game in another part of town. This adventure caused some to wonder if there was life for Motown after this hit-making machine made their dramatic move.

Let's face it. HDH was really a huge entity at Motown. Many people felt their abrupt departure would impact the success of Motown and it was necessary to think of alternative survival tactics.

It did indeed impact Motown. One group in particular was the Four Tops. When the team left, the Tops lost some of their steam and signed with ABC when their contract was up for re-signing. The Supremes felt the pinch as well.

This team of songwriters was awesome. After a brief interval (maybe a year) HDH had a new address and the music industry was witnessing the inception of Hot Wax/Invictus Record Company.

What about musicians for this new company?

You guessed it. They called on the Funk Brothers. Those three geniuses knew that we were an essential part of the formula that made the hits. The news of us cutting dates for HDH quickly reached the Motown offices. They employed camera crews to film us going into the HDH Studio.

Were we important or what? The stars didn't have camera crews following them.

The studio itself was an old converted movie theater, located on Grand River Avenue. The crannies also disguised themselves and filmed from across the street in parked cars, behind trash cans, in vacant buildings, behind bushes, and filmed us like they were doing a movie. These pictures would go directly to Berry. This kind of harassment continued on for weeks and weeks at a time. Does this sound like company procedure for a record establishment or had we escaped from the Gestapo?

Of course we were not fired, but we were 'punished' in various ways for recording sessions 'away from home'.

Invictus was charged with a profusion of electrifying creativity. HDH continued to collaborate and the hits just kept on coming. They produced acts like Freda Payne ('Band of Gold'), Chairmen of the Board ('Patches') Glass House, The Honey Cone and a few others.

We were taking care of plenty business cutting almost every day. The group was augmented with the addition of Dennis Coffey, Bob Babbitt, Ray Parker Jr, Wah-Wah Watson, Robert White, Jack Brokensha, Johnny Griffith, Pistol Allen, Sylvester Rivers, Eddie Bongo, Eddie Willis, Uriel Jones, James Jamerson, and Earl Van Dyke. McKinley Jackson did most of the arranging and sometimes they used Sylvester Rivers. Lawrence Horn was the chief engineer. Ronnie Dunbar was a very loyal assistant.

Motown was striking out more and more against some of the musicians because now they had proof from the 'Camera Crew' that we were cutting at Invictus. The atmosphere at Invictus was filled with uneasiness and suspicions. We could feel their eyes staring us down to see if we had any kind of paraphernalia that we could use against them. I had never worked in a studio with a one way mirrored control room. Sometimes you didn't know if you were going to the studio to cut a session or to be interrogated. And under no circumstances were you to ask questions. We worked under a lot of duress and pressure, but HDH felt the heat as well.

One time on a Chairmen of the Board session, I had a camera in my bag. I would often take a lot of pictures of the musicians and this was just one of those times. I took a picture of Eddie Bongo reading a girlie magazine (his favorite).

When the camera flashed, the paranoid producers and engineers converged upon me as though I was a criminal.

They demanded, "Turn over that camera, NOW! You can't take pictures in here!"

I clearly understood what they said, but I honestly thought they were kidding, so I put the camera back into my bag.

Eddie Holland yelled, "We gotta have that picture, 'cause you might be taking it back to Berry."

In total disbelief, I couldn't get the words out quick enough: "Why, tell me, why would Berry want a picture of Eddie Bongo reading a magazine taken with a two dollar camera, when there's a whole camera crew outside, with pictures of everyone that has come in here for the last month? Can you answer that question?"

No one had an answer. They just looked at me and instructed me to follow. We all marched into the control room like I was being arrested for stealing. Eddie Holland explained in a very business like tone, "I have to call my attorney for advice."

I looked at Eddie Bongo with total disgust because the claim was so bogus.

Eddie Holland got his attorney on the phone and began detailing what had happened. "Hello Fred, Eddie Holland here. We've got a serious problem with a musician snapping pictures here in the studio. What should we do?" He hung up the phone and said, "You've got to wait here for our attorney." He ordered his assistants to "lock all of the doors."

With arms outstretched I asked, "So are you going to keep me in here against my will?" HDH sessions represented a large portion of my income and I didn't want to show my true anger for fear of destroying our working relationship. Bongo even tried to persuade them to drop the senseless claim: "Man we take pictures on sessions all the time. Jack ain't no snitch."

Eddie Holland very cautiously explained, "We'll just have to wait for our attorney to tell us what to do."

The attorney arrived and immediately began stating a lot of legal terms and attempting to condemn me for something I wasn't guilty of.

"Listen, your fight is not with me, it's with Berry Gordy. I'm all for you and this company. I'm in your cheering section. You can have the film, get it developed and you'll see that it was just a picture of Bongo that I took," I explained. The expression on his face revealed that he felt he had been called in for nothing. He reluctantly accepted the film and HDH seemed satisfied.

I left the studio a little angry but I realized that Berry's boys had basically upset everybody, snooping and intimidating the operations of Invictus.

From Motown's vantage point, to get a clearer picture of the musicians outside sessions, what could be better than to have a Funk Brother to become an 'undercover agent'? So Johnny Griffith was approached and he accepted the job.

He was put on a weekly salary to inform the Motown flunkies of any outside sessions that the Motown musicians might be doing. He was to tell who was on them and who the producer was.

Johnny would be called in from time to time to give reports. He would tell them that he had nothing to report. After so many times of having nothing to report, he was fired from his 'spy job'.

Then there was another Sherlock assigned to do the same job as Johnny Griffith. It was Eddie Willis on the payroll this time. The results were the same – nothing to report and no sessions.

I want to make it clear, the Funk Brothers were loyal to each other and anyone thinking differently was absolutely crazy. I remember a couple of occasions when Hank Cosby and Ralph Seltzer came slinking into a session wearing pajamas and night caps, and caught us cutting a date for an outside client. They thought that they had really scared us by showing their faces at the sessions and making idle threats.

I'm sure you are wondering why there was such a big fuss about the Funks cutting outside dates.

This is how I see it. We were the best musicians around that were able to give a producer the best sounds on the tracks. We were experienced and very easy to work with. It seldom took more than one or two takes and the producers had just what they wanted on tape.

By playing on outside dates, Berry was afraid that he would lose the distinction we gave his company. He feared that Motown's impressive position at the top of Billboard's charts would plummet to rock bottom, if some other company gained access to our skills.

He was likely correct, but we were not compensated to be exclusive artists, given royalties, or offered any monetary payments. We just wanted to play music and make money doing so. When we had the opportunity to cut a session for companies other than Motown, we had no reason whatsoever to turn down work.

With HDH defecting from Motown, it afforded Norman Whitfield an opportunity to advance and that's exactly what he did. I did a session for Norman at Studio A during this time, and he had someone superimpose his face on a picture that depicted him as Superman.

Since HDH had left the building he did appear to be a Superman for real.

There is one thing that I can truly say about Brian, Eddie, and Lamont. These guys were always friendly and genuinely nice to the musicians while at Motown, as well as when they were at Invictus. Some of the producers had a tendency to think that they were better than the musicians, and looked down on us. But this wasn't the case with HDH. They had the resources but never tried to flaunt their wealth. Eddie Holland had a Stutz Bearcat automobile, Brian had a racehorse, and they all had beautiful homes. Their names became synonymous with number one hits, gold and platinum. Everybody loved Holland-Dozier-Holland because they were genuine talent and true gentlemen.

ALL ABOUT THE FUNK BROTHERS

We lived as one. By us playing in the clubs at night and then playing in the day at the sessions, we would sometimes do innovative things that weren't written on a chart. In fact most of what we did in sessions wasn't written out. It was the stuff we played the night before that we would play on the sessions. Earl would say something like, "Hey, do that song we did that last night, Jack. Play the intro and see how it fits."

"Okay .. Bam!" It would fit like a glove and sound like the parts were written out on the charts.

Motown wasn't a blues company and we didn't play the blues. That's why the things we did sounded so good. The changes and the moves that we made rhythmically were very hip.

As Motown came to dominate the pop charts and several of the acts became household names, the Funk Brothers who pumped life into the songs remained nameless and without recognition. We knew we were hot and we knew we were good. But the general consensus was that they would downplay our importance to avoid us from getting a representative to attempt to cut a recording deal for the Funks.

If we had done that, it would be a different story today. When the Funks weren't hard at work in Studio A, we were jamming at the Chit Chat Lounge on 12th Street. We all played jazz, and that's what we played at the club. The Chit Chat was an incredible place. It was the hottest spot to go to during the early sixties. It was common to see Smokey Robinson, The Temptations, or any of the Motown acts that were in between tours or gigs.

After the riots it was one of the only buildings left standing. That's because the community accepted the proprietor and really liked him.

"The Funk Brothers were the band of life," said Smokey Robinson.

The band of life? Those are pretty powerful words from a very reliable person. That was generally how most people felt about our music, but we were never told by the top administrators.

In spite of all not credited to our great contributions, our lingering legacy will survive, and it will always remain through many future decades. We set a precedent in the annals of music that will always exist. We brought about a change in music, and a change in society.

ALL ABOUT THE FUNK BROTHERS

If God blessed Berry Gordy for making it happen, then the angels kissed the Funk Brothers for furthering his dream. Without the Funk Brothers, there would have been no Motown.

Robert White, one of the two guitarists, started out at Motown working at a little studio that Berry's sister Anna operated on St Antoine Street. He stayed busy cutting gospel songs while developing his arranging skills. He demonstrated exceptional talent as an arranger, but was constantly overlooked.

Eventually, he maneuvered his way into Studio A on West Grand Boulevard. Robert fraternized with Earl Van Dyke more than any of the other Funk Brothers.

Robert was beneficial in helping to make sure that my jazz influence in music didn't conflict with the 'funky' way studio musicians played. He often reminded me to "Just keep it simple." We all worked together on the club scene and bonded as friends.

Frankly, it was more than just friendship. We were not connected biologically, but we were genuine brothers and brought a new meaning to the word brotherhood. Our relationship didn't require a daily confirmation. The camaraderie that existed between us was anchored in love and trust.

Robert was thought of by most as being serious minded and the brain of the group. None of us was dumb or illiterate, and we were all pretty clever with words. With Robert, sometimes, the depth of his conversation required you to do some serious brainwork or what he was saying would go right over your head. He was a philosopher and loved to indulge in debating topics.

A few months after I arrived in Detroit, I needed a TV and at that time I didn't have any credit. I expressed my problem to Robert and he offered to assist by co-signing for me. He made it known that it wasn't an everyday practice to chance his good credit rating, but he wanted to befriend me and we worked together.

That was very special, and I never forgot him for that favor and the trust he had in me. Of course I paid him back quickly, and our friendship continued on. Robert had a very kind spirit and always displayed his concern for others. What he did for me, he probably would have done for someone else.

Like a few of the other guys Robert would smoke pot, but he never had a drug problem. He believed that "the herb from the earth's soil was good for man's soul." That was one of his philosophies. He never tried to impose his philosophy or beliefs on anyone.

Early on, I recognized Robert's talents as an arranger and utilized his skills on an album I recorded in Los Angeles, California. It was a film score entitled *Blackjack*.

Robert's talents on this project were absolutely superb. He played on the tracks as well as arranged the tunes. I listened to his flawless and innovative arrangements over and over and imagined what the apex of his career could have been. His signature performance on 'My Girl' will stand undisputed as the most famous four bars probably ever recorded.

Richard 'Pistol' Allen, drummer extraordinaire, was a native of Memphis, Tennessee. He left Memphis and lived in Flint, Michigan before joining Motown.

Pistol was a very warm and friendly guy who loved jazz music. He performed as a Motown studio musician and worked the jazz circuits at night. You would seldom see Pistol without some kind of cap or hat on. He was known for being able to read a racing form and never miss a beat while playing the drums. He always kept tabs on the horses.

He never tried to hide the fact that in spite of him already knowing how to play the drums, Bennie Benjamin taught him how to be a Motown recording musician.

Whenever jazz groups would come to Detroit, that's where you would find Pistol. That would usually be at Baker's Keyboard Lounge, located at Livernois and Eight Mile Road. He would hang out with guys like Sonny Stitt and Coltrane. He always knew when these guys would be appearing.

Pistol was the father of ten children and several grandchildren.

His battle with lung cancer ended on June 30, 2002. Again, the Funks lost another link in our chain.

The happiness he displayed while filming the documentary was absolutely indescribable and that's how I remember him. He was sick a couple of times on the set, but like a warrior he pressed on and never wavered. I was too bereaved to attend the final service.

Stevie Wonder, Martha Reeves, Paul Riser, Berry Gordy's sister Esther Gordy, and several others were in attendance. On that day, July 5, 2002, I reflected on the recent times I had spoken with him and all of the good times we shared. I knew that this day was inevitable, but I still prayed that God would allow him to enjoy his accomplishments. It just wasn't meant to be. He made it to the finish line and wasn't able to cross over. So close, yet so far away. That's the part that continues to grieve our hearts. We miss him and speak of his legacy quite often.

Bennie Benjamin was what some called the greatest drummer to ever record for Motown. He was best known for his impeccable timing and unique 'pick-ups'.

That awful day in 1968 when he passed away was enough to close the company down. The words from Earl echoed into my telephone "Jack, Bennie is dead! Jack, Bennie is dead!"

"Oh my God! No!" I yelled in disbelief. This sad news tore me apart with intense heartfelt sadness. His star had just begun to rise. His unusual pick-ups and rhythm were gaining lots of attention, and fans as well as other musicians would listen for his unique flavoring on the tracks.

I always wanted to say or do something to help him pull away from his self-destructive lifestyle. He would just smile at my advice and say "I'm OK, man and I thank you for your concern."

He never ceased to amaze us with his hilarious excuses regarding why he would be late for a session. One of his best excuses was, he was stuck in traffic on Woodward Avenue because an elephant broke loose from a circus wagon and traffic came to a standstill. Of course we knew that wasn't true because Bennie didn't drive, and he most definitely didn't own a car.

I combed the newspaper for Bennie's funeral arrangements. A few names down from the top of the obituary column was Bennie's name.

I sent a floral design and prepared myself to see all of the Motown folks sitting around the coffin saying how much they loved and respected him. Norman Whitfield, Blinkie Williams, and the Funk Brothers were the only ones from Motown. There was a sea of beautiful floral arrangements placed around the church.

While Bennie's body rested still and lifeless, I stood peering over him praying for his soul. I stared at him and touched his cold hand. I felt he was at peace.

Unknown to anyone, I slipped a tambourine cymbal under his hand. The reason for doing that was that in 1964 we were recording 'Going To A Go-Go' and his drumstick hit my tambourine and knocked one of the cymbals off.

He told me, "As long as you keep that cymbal in your life, you'll be successful." So I wanted to give it back to him so he could be successful on his journey home.

The Funks felt downhearted and traumatized. Seemingly nothing could be said to lessen the blow. Norman Whitfield offered his sympathy and encouraged us to continue on harder now than ever. "Bennie is now free, and you guys should be happy for him." Norman was a different kind of a guy.

After his sympathetic expressions, we walked away together and he told me that he wanted me to play on his session the following week. I told him I would come but there were a couple of people I would like to avoid. He assured me that it didn't matter and all I needed to do was show up and play. He declared: "On my stuff, I need the tambourine and I need you, because you are the best that ever did it."

I met him at the studio along with the other Funks and we cut Edwin Starr's 'War'. Norman was quite elated about the resulting sound as well as my return to studio A. It had been eighteen months since I stepped on Motown's property. It was during this time that Mike and I had opened Pied Piper Productions on Livernois near Joy Road.

Norman began spreading the news: "Jack is back!"

Frank Wilson heard what I had done on Norman's production and wanted me to do some recording for him. Beside being a good producer, Frank was one of the nicest producers that I had ever worked with. He was a perfect gentleman and I really liked working with him. I was 'back in the saddle again', and I give Norman all of the credit for that.

Uriel Jones, like me, first went to Motown by way of the Marvin Gaye tour. He became a part of the rhythm section with us at Motown in 1963. He was a very 'funky' drummer and the Motown producers loved him. In spite of already having two drummers beating out rhythms, Uriel was added as a third drummer. Remarkably they never got in the way of each other.

In the early sixties, Uriel toured with Marvin Gaye and later with Earl Van Dyke. Uriel acquired a comfortable lifestyle with his boat and his horses. He had several riding horses that he kept and rode in Windsor, Canada with his friends. Many times he would leave a gig and go directly to his boat.

Like the other Funks Uriel spoke our private language very well. Other people didn't understand what we were saying but it was very funny. We sounded like we were speaking a dialect of 'Pig Latin'.

Uriel had a great sense of humor and could easily match wits with Eddie Bongo or anyone else.

Eddie Willis' playing had a southern soulful feel to it and that's because he learned to play in Mississippi where he was born. Eddie was one of the first to record at Motown in 1959. He did a lot of work on the road, touring with the Marvelettes, and spent almost two decades playing all over the world with the Four Tops.

Eddie was physically challenged during the early years of his life, but it never infringed on his talented playing and recording. Eddie has always been a very likeable guy who never had a lot to say. He was one of the quiet guys of the group. We always deeply admired him for his strong will and determination.

His legendary guitar licks on 'The Way You Do The Things You Do' will forever live in the hearts of millions. His musical influences were Chet Atkins, Wes Montgomery, and Albert King.

Joe Messina was not characterized because he was a Caucasian, but because of his flawless guitar licks. His back-beats were heard on almost every release.

Joe was a local jazz guitarist who played nationally on the Soupy Sales show. He was challenged on almost every session to double James Jamerson's bass line. Joe was actually recruited by Berry Gordy.

When the company closed, in spite of the fact that Berry brought him into the company, he was left behind with the other Funks. Joe was a very quiet guy who always had a big pleasant smile.

I think sometimes he would wonder how we thought up so much to laugh about. He would laugh at the fun things we did, but never joined in. Joe played mostly Italian music before going to Motown in 1959. After being exposed to the world on the Soupy Sales Show, he had the opportunity of playing with John Coltrane, Charlie Parker, and other jazz greats that were guest artists on the show.

There were three names at Motown that were often confused. They were Ivy Hunter, Ivory Joe Hunter, and Joe Hunter.

Joe Hunter was the first Funk Brother to record with Motown. His talented fingers turned out some 'earthy, down home' piano playing. He's heard clearly on 'Pride and Joy', 'Come and Get these Memories', and that all time great hit 'Heat Wave'.

Joe learned to first play the piano simply by listening to another family member play. Finding it much to his liking he took piano lessons in his hometown, Jackson, Tennessee. Joe, like the other Funks, played around town in the clubs at night. His work was sort of 'squeezed out' by Earl Van Dyke, because of Earl's dominance on the keyboard. Joe kept us entertained with Shakespearean quotes and passages from Broadway plays.

Currently in his mid-70s, Joe still performs full time throughout the Detroit metropolitan area. His musical influences were Art Tatum, Sergei Rachmaninov and Nat King Cole.

Johnny Griffith was one of the few classically trained musicians. He came to Motown in 1961 hoping to record a jazz album. He did record an album, but Motown needed his perfect touch to accompany Earl Van Dyke as a second pianist. Through all of his recording on rhythm and blues sessions, he always remained a jazz hopeful.

Johnny had a good business aptitude and flaunted his vocabulary to make some of the administrators fear or recruit him. He ended up being Hitsville's hired gun. He was paid a salary to report any outside activity about the Funks playing on someone else's dates.

Johnny accepted the money, but his loyalty was with us and he reported to Mickey Stevenson "I saw nothing." That went on for a while until they found out their Sherlock was just taking their money and reporting absolutely nothing.

Johnny was born in Detroit and spent most of his life there. His musical idols were Bud Powell, Glenn Gould and Oscar Peterson.

Bob Babbitt was born in Pittsburg, Pennsylvania as Robert Kreinar. Babbitt is a nickname that caught on and was adopted by everybody.

He worked in the shadows of James Jamerson, but was still able to assert his own style and identity.

After freelancing around Detroit in the early sixties, Bob joined Stevie Wonder's band in 1966 and eventually was brought into the studio in 1967. He was needed as a second bassist to do the work Jamerson wasn't able to do.

Babbitt was instantly accepted into the Funk Brothers' fraternity. The stage was set when Bob played on some of the tracks from Marvin Gaye's *What's Going On?* album.

After the doors were closed in Detroit in 1972, Bob stayed busy doing studio work in New York, Philadelphia, and Nashville.

Color was never an issue with him, the Funks or the fans that loved him. He gained great recognition for his excellence and superiority on 'Signed, Sealed, Delivered', and 'War'.

Eddie 'Bongo' Brown was born in Memphis, Tennessee, and like so many others migrated to Detroit looking for better job opportunities. He knew that he wanted to further his musical career but didn't have a reasonable outlet. There were bands seeking piano players or bass players, but seldom a bongo or conga player.

He was first Marvin Gaye's valet and later became Hitsville's most prolific conga player, embellishing the tracks of 'Cloud Nine', 'What's Going On', 'Beauty Is Only Skin Deep', and many, many more.

Eddie was a true comedian in every sense of the word. His ability to 'play the dozens' was remarkable. His instant comedy lines could have qualified him for a sit-com. Eddie kept everybody rolling with laughter. Eddie's musical influence was Chano Pozo.

Earl Van Dyke and James Jamerson were probably the most remembered. Their contributions were quite prominent.

Actually, each of us in our own way were respected musicians. We were comparable to war troops who 'took to the hills despite the heavy enemy fire'. Our 'war stories' and 'wounds' have left indelible marks upon our hearts, but we've climbed those insurmountable hills and lived with our legacies quietly, alone, and unknown.

THE CLOSING OF MOTOWN AND ITS DOMINO EFFECT

Motown Records is a company name as recognizable as General Motors. However, the guys who played on the tracks went nameless, and without recognition. They performed on an undetermined number of chartbusters that kept the fans dancing and moving. The Four Tops, The Supremes, The Temptations, Gladys Knight and The Pips – and the list goes on and on. Everybody knew those acts and bought their records, and probably thought each act had their own band. Guess what? It was us, the Funks. We played on everybody's tracks. Maybe we didn't get our proper recognition but it is unanimously agreed that Motown's success was attributed a lot to its musicians. Berry stood as the head of this exceptional dynasty and made the mark of excellence in this musical era.

In 1959, this musical giant, Berry Gordy, decided to forego his interest in boxing to pursue songwriting. Destiny had already secretly launched circumstances that would produce the most distinguished music tycoon known to the music industry. His wizardry and leadership is comparable to Moses leading his people out of the desert and across the Red Sea.

His calculated risk has steered many from rags to riches. With only $800 and a calculated dream, Motown Records was born. Berry's eye for talent and his golden ears made him an exceptional chance taker who had dreams of becoming a record maker.

Upon the inception of Tamla/Motown, I'm certain this visionary had never dreamed that his company would reach the staggering heights it did achieve. Its cataclysmic impact will be echoed in the future for hundreds of years, in turn making the men that played the music immortal souls.

There were a few releases right after the inception of Motown, but Marv Johnson's 'Come To Me' really gave the company its first big hit. It swept the country, and carved the way for many other artists to tread.

For decades this legendary place called Hitsville USA has cranked out what seemed effortlessly many number one hits. Sometimes the Motown releases swallowed up all of the top spots on the Billboard charts. This phenomenon was never matched or repeated.

And now the big question. How could a company of this magnitude ever think of moving? Or even worse, how could this establishment close its doors and move to another city?

No one had assumed or speculated that this would actually happen. Whether we (the studio musicians/Funk Brothers) were naïve or captured in a net of false security, we were benumbed when this actually happened.

As the company rapidly grew from its meager beginnings to the days when I was a recording musician, on any given day you could bump into Smokey Robinson, The Miracles, The Four Tops, Gladys Knight and the Pips, The Temptations, The Supremes, Stevie Wonder, or any artist on the Motown roster. Hitsville's doors were always opened to the 'family'. Artists would drop in for any number of reasons. Sometimes during the warm season it was commonplace to see some of these acts sitting out on the front porch and steps. It was a beehive of activities. I can remember when producers like Holland-Dozier-Holland, Norman Whitfield, and Johnny Bristol would be in line to cut a session. Sometimes we would record for three or four different producers back to back.

As the 'family' atmosphere seemed to 'slightly vanish', Berry started becoming less visible. The 'grapevine' had it that the reason why he wasn't frequently seen was because he spent a great deal of time in Los Angeles.

When Holland-Dozier-Holland ventured on their own, you might say that the storm clouds were slowly moving in. No thunder or lightning yet .. maybe .. just maybe .. nothing to fear.

There were little signs but nothing concrete at this point. The administration department was now in the Donovan Building and much of the business Berry conducted was from LA by phone. The hits were still happening but not with the trust that was once there. Berry's vision seemed more and more fixed on the West Coast, Diana, and the movie industry.

With just a few scattered facts I wondered if anything would be enough to close the doors of Hitsville. Berry's untiring attention was all basically on Diana. Naturally this made the other female artists feel abandoned and dejected. The Jackson Five had signed with another company and that took a big chunk out of the company. U-m-m-m, would that be the deciding factor of the company's future?

The musicians were cutting not quite as much, but we were working often in the 'Snake Pit'. The Funk Brothers and other musicians were never privy to any administrative matters.

When circumstances surfaced it was usually old news. As a rule we seldom visited the Donovan Building, and for some ungodly reason the artists were given special orders to avoid the musicians.

We were oblivious to what was going on. I agree that Motown may have had its problems, but didn't anyone have the foresight to have an East Coast operation as well as a West Coast operation? Didn't Hitsville have the proven magic that made this company high above the average? Why? Why? Why?

Everybody asks this question: why did Motown/Hitsville shut down in Detroit in 1973 and declare LA (Mowest) its headquarters?

This question had been asked as much as who assassinated President Kennedy. There's never been a committee to investigate the Motown saga, but 'inquiring minds' want to know. That's not really being unreasonable; people just want to know. It may very well not be anybody's business except Berry Gordy's, but the fans and followers as well as the people that worked at Motown would love to have an explanation signed and stamped 'VALID'.

Bear with me as I rewind my mental tape and convey how those unforgettable moments took place in my life.

The distasteful news of the closedown stood in sharp contrast to what I was expecting. We were scheduled to do a session at the 'Snake Pit'. I drove to the studio and there stood James Jamerson, Eddie Bongo, and Earl Van Dyke assembled at the door.

"Hey, fellows, what's going on?" I greeted them as I usually did.

The response was dry, dull, and slow. I quickly knew that this indicated that something was wrong.

I asked, "What's wrong? Did somebody die?" Earl just looked at me and pointed to the sign on the door that read: 'Today's session is cancelled and will be rescheduled'.

OK I can live with that. So what? The session has been cancelled and will be rescheduled. There was just one thing that bothered me. I peeped in the window and the lobby was dark and appeared abandoned. I jokingly said, "It looks like they moved out." My personal radar antennas ascended immediately with that chilling thought.

I wondered about the circumstances much more than I expressed. We talked for a few moments and decided to go on home.

"Call me and let me know if you hear anything," I said, with concern in my voice.

Earl assured me, "Man, you know they will be calling us in a day or two."

Well, several days passed and there was no word from anyone. We called Motown, but no one answered the telephone. That was unusual. Eddie Bongo went downtown to the Motown office building (the Donovan Building on Woodward Avenue). He called me from there and sounded like he was about to hit the panic button. "Jack! You won't believe what I'm about to tell you. There are several moving companies with big vans, moving *everything* out of the Donovan Building. Everybody's gone! You ain't go' believe this s---."

This unbelievable account sounded like Eddie had 'flown the coop'.

"Are you sure that all of this is going on?" I inquired. He barely had time to answer before I grabbed my car keys, drove to the corner and hit the expressway located right in back of my house, doing about a hundred, heading in the direction of downtown. I was there in less than fifteen minutes.

On the way there, my mind reverted back to a couple of years ago after finishing a Martha Reeves session when I asked the question, "Suppose all of this action would close down one day?"

I don't know why I asked that question, but there were no answers. The guys just looked at me as though I had just jumped over my own shadow.

That fifteen minute drive seemed endless and a smorgasbord of questions raced through my mind. Who wrote the note at the Studio? Why were movers moving everything from the building? Who authorized the move? Where is everybody? And why in the hell didn't somebody notify the musicians?

'Bean-Bolski' (the nickname James Jamerson gave Eddie) was waiting for me out front. The building security was tight and we couldn't enter any one of the several doors. Most of the offices had been cleared and there were absolutely no familiar faces exiting. As the furniture was being moved we managed to ask the movers a few questions.

"Where is all of this furniture going?"

"Where is everybody that once worked here?"

"We don't know," and one mover got a little belligerent saying "Would you like me to repeat that? – WE DON'T KNOW!"

They were very tight-lipped and according to them they knew nothing.

It is common among friends to say that 'seeing is believing'. But even seeing with my own eyes I felt some measure of doubt that this was really taking place. The questions continued to roll over and over in my mind. How could Motown move out of the city and leave the guys that made the music behind and never say a word? Is Motown out of business? How could anyone fry the goose that had been laying the golden eggs? (Or in this case, golden records.) If you didn't understand that metaphor, I was brainstorming the idea of Berry closing his company that was doing quite well. This was a mind-blowing experience. For the life of me I just couldn't make sense of it all. The whole thing seemed like a farce. The stream of movers continued to empty the building as Bongo and I just stood around witnessing the 'Musical Wheels of Motown' come to a screeching halt. We wore the breast plate of sadness and at that moment my vision became blurred with tears.

"Oh well, we had a good run, didn't we?" I said.

We finally went home and began to try think of ways to carve out our futures. I thought about my financial responsibilities. Would I have the money to pay the house note, car note and could I adequately provide for my wife and child? Since I relocated to Detroit I had never had to face any financial trauma.

We all had our opinions about what happened. The telephones were buzzing hot gossip all over Detroit and the West Coast too.

"Did you hear about Motown shutting down?"

"Did you hear that Berry Gordy sold Motown?"

"Did you hear that the Martians have taken over Motown?" This move was like the impact of General Motors with its gargantuan operation shutting down.

To make it even clearer about the way Motown left Detroit, I would say it was comparable to someone running into a crowded auditorium screaming, "FIRE! FIRE!" You know what happens when someone yells fire. The building empties almost instantly. Motown's unparalleled circumstance made the most uncaring person stop and wonder about what happened. Even people that didn't work there felt like they had been stripped of a precious jewel that gave the city a special flair. Motown was Detroit's child and was supported by the entire city. Its closing sent shock waves around the country.

When we were recording for Motown, we would quietly do outside sessions, but were very dependent upon the Motown producers to call us as the main source of our income. So what did I do now when the colossal effects of Motown moving to California had been felt? I didn't know exactly what, but I knew I had to do something to counteract and withstand the pressure of the days ahead.

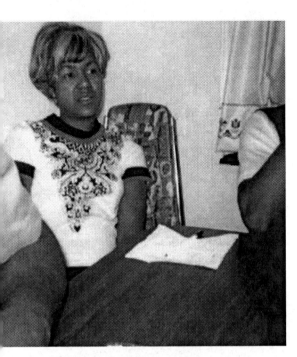

Billie Jean Brown – June 1969

Fran Heard – Motown tape librarian, 1964

Johnny Mae Matthews with the Funk Brothers at a Detroit club.

On tour with Marvin Gaye in
July, 1964

(above) With Mike Terry, 1965

(left) With Marvin's wife, Anna in 1964

(below) With Marvin at the 'Got To Give It Up' session, 1975

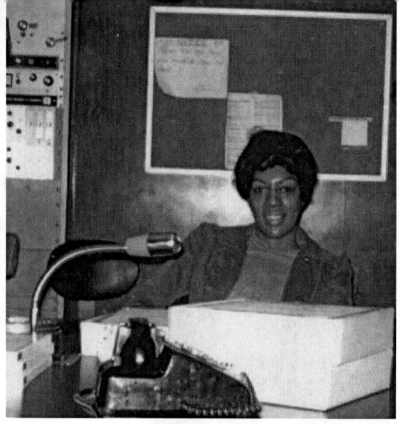

Lorraine Chandler at the Motown studio, 1971

Barbara Terry

Freddie Butler with James Jamerson and Clifford Mack.

The Spinners with (front row) Pervis Jackson,
Eli Fontaine and me.

Char with top Motown arranger, Paul Riser

Sam Moore from Sam and Dave outside
Muscle Shoals studios

September, 1971 – Sam and Dave with
session musicians and producers, Dave
Crawford and Barry Beckett.

THE CLOSING OF MOTOWN

Actually, the shut down hurled a set of circumstances in our lives that was bigger than BIG. Nobody had prepared or was ready for this insensitive change. There had been a few whispers that a change would one day come but everybody considered it to be propaganda. Trying to sell the idea of Motown moving to a loyal company employee (and they were all loyal) would have been like trying to sell a snow-plow in the desert. Furthermore, they would have become very hostile at such a thought. Were we blind? Not exactly. We were blissfully reconciled to the way things were – the good life, plenty of money, nice homes, nice cars, etc.

The musicians and I kept in close contact with each other. With the 'Snake Pit' closed the dialog shared between us was focused on any work we may have heard about around town or with Jamerson. He was heading for Los Angeles. He felt he might be able to do better there than in Detroit. It wasn't clear if he had been promised work, or if his $100,000 guaranteed annual salary had been cancelled.

His potential seemed better than the other Funks because Berry had at one time seemed to play favoritism with him.

In 1973, he took off to Los Angeles. After arriving there, he was slapped in the face with the fact that other bass players had been recording, and he was in competition with the West Coast musicians.

His counterparts were on Ben Barrett's call list. That made all the difference in the world. The news of Jamerson living in LA was well circulated but he didn't receive the expected response. The calls came from just a few producers that had used him on dates in Detroit. The roster of musicians had changed completely, and left little room for penetration.

For instance, Earl Van Dyke and Johnny Griffith were used on keyboards in Detroit. Greg Phillinganes and Joe Sample were used on keyboards in LA Eddie Willis, Robert White and Joe Messina were used in Detroit. David T. Walker, Paul Jackson, and Wah-Wah Watson were used in LA. This is just an example of how things changed.

Motown had releases, but most without the distinctive and superior bass playing of James Jamerson. Bass players tried to emulate his style on sessions, but fell way short of doing so. Believe me, anyone that played bass anywhere knew that his style was the style most sought after. I'm not trying to say there were no hits after being isolated, but the magnitude of record sales was way down and the artists were leaving and signing with other companies for various reasons.

Motown's West Coast operation was distinctively differentiated from Detroit's MO. James, I'm sure, would have preferred the comfort and security of a contract from Motown, but I was told at this time he was a free agent. His freedom allowed him to move about the industry freely to record and tour, as well as record sessions for ads and jingles, movie scores, and do recording for various artists.

He made money and seemed to have been doing well. He would call back to Detroit and express how much he missed playing with all of the Funks, and how he really missed his family. He would say things like, "This is a foreign land out here and everybody is a big phony. I just can't lock in to what these musicians are playing."

What they were playing was called the 'new sound' or 'slapping'. No matter what the other musicians were playing, Jamerson was going to play his style, and the new trends in bass playing (slapping and popping strings) would have to proceed without him. He could have adapted to the new style of playing but that would have been like asking him to try to sound like everybody else, when some of these guys for years had been trying to sound like him.

What a blow! James had a brush with violence during a robbery in 1981 that resulted in a severed artery, but nothing hurt him as profoundly as the manner in which he was treated in LA.

No matter how much he abused himself with drinks and drugs I firmly believe he died of a broken heart.

With the 'Changing of the Guard' so to speak, Jamerson's calls for work became less and less. Some people would have you to believe that Jamerson had turned into a flame-throwing, out-of-control beast, whose fingers would lock instead of gliding over the strings of his instruments. They said that's why he was given the 'cold shoulder' and ousted.

Some people may not know that Jamerson's favorite drink was Metaxa and for the purpose of getting 'bombed' he also smoked weed. He never had a warehouse of drugs that he loaded up on daily and was usually pleasant until he felt wronged.

His playing ability was fantastic as late as 1980. I have the tapes that he played on, and he never missed a lick.

His depression (in my opinion) was the result of the changeover of Motown and the cold treatment he received in LA.

That was difficult for any of us to understand. We felt robbed and betrayed. If I were a drinking man or a drug user, I just might have ended up in a rehab clinic.

Earl Van Dyke thought the grounds of LA were more fertile for studio work. He anticipated getting a decent amount of keyboard work or at least enough to support him and his family. Here again, Joe Sample, John Barnes, Sonny Burke, and Greg Phillinganes were all on Ben Barrett's call list. The drudgery meant little to those who were in power and they made no efforts to call Earl or Jamerson. The suggestion by Jamerson for Earl to go to LA proved to be far from the desired outcome.

With both Earl and Jamerson in the same city, it was automatically assumed by the two that they would be playing in somebody's studio, on somebody's session together at one time or another. That was not to be. They missed it. No one had the 'thunder' on the piano like Earl. Somebody making the calls to musicians to work needed a behavioral scientist to keep them straight on the selections.

Earl's persistent attitude and strong will to win gave him the ammunition to press on in spite of being rejected. He joined forces with Freda Payne and toured successfully with her.

With Earl leaving Detroit, that prompted a move also for Robert White and Eddie Bongo. Just as pioneers years ago traveled to the west in pursuit of gold, the Funks' path bore a resemblance in their pursuance of survival in the music industry. The recording dates were few and the Funks kept 'running into brick walls'. Doors were slammed into the faces of musical legends. Like farm crops suffering from a period of serious drought, these Funks were suffering as the studio work simply 'dried up' and diminished.

Earl called me one day and told me, "We have been shut out from session dates, and I'll starve if I stay out here. I'll be getting back to Detroit soon."

"What do you think happened?" I asked.

"Well, you know that I didn't forget how to play keyboards. It's just a new group that has taken over out here, and these guys are getting all of the work. Ben Barrett has his preferred list of musicians that does not include me."

Soon after that phone call, Earl returned to Detroit and began teaching music in the Detroit public school system. Was that any place for this musical giant to be tucked away in? It really wasn't the best place for him, but he did adapt, and he did it very well.

The failure of Earl's attempts to penetrate the iron walls of Ben

Barrett's internal operation should have sent an unmistakable message that the Funk Brothers were no longer in demand as we were in Detroit. The average person would have crumbled and felt defeated, but the Funks were steadfast and immovable from the music we so dearly loved. We had to press on with unremitting efforts to avoid perishing.

We tried to acquire any work that existed with any producer. Eddie Bongo would call producers almost daily, and travel from studio to studio. He would hang out at the Musicians Union like he had a job there. He would talk to different producers and arrangers about calling him for a session. He left no stone unturned. Sometimes he would go to a session like he had been called to play on it. King Erickson and Paulinho Da Costa were being called instead of Eddie. Neither of these guys outplayed him, but Da Costa put on a good show.

In Robert's case, his chance for session dates was so minimal that he moved from LA proper to a small town in California. Robert's approach to life was guided by his Religion, Eckancar. He was a deeper thinker and usually made decisions as a result of his mediation and prayers. So I suppose that the decision to move was guided by the wisdom and principles of his religion. I corresponded with him from time to time, and he made it known that he was not happy away from music.

I kept in closer contact with Eddie 'Bongo' probably than any one else. Our contact was by phone and we would talk about some of everything. He would try to keep me abreast of the happenings in LA and never failed to say, "Come on out man, we're waiting for you."

I had earned the reputation of being like the Biblical character Job, who displayed remarkable patience. I wasn't quick to move and let go of what I had, and moving would take some serious thought. I had to reason with these circumstances.

I resided just a minute from the very studio that I once recorded in almost daily. It was now closed. I had a wife and two little girls to feed and my savings had become infinitesimal. I had remained in Detroit attempting to make a last ditch effort to find something to keep me busy in order to make a living.

I honestly didn't want to go to LA. On the other hand I was approaching the eleventh hour, with little time to debate. The move was indicated, but I tried to avoid it as long as I could.

I borrowed money from Paul Riser to make some mortgage payments and stay afloat. Things were just bad. I entertained the idea of becoming a factory worker since I lived in the Motor City, but music was in my blood. If I had to stand and fight, I'd rather do it where there was some recording business going on. Sure the Motown era had closed but there were a lot of other attempts by other producers at several studios in 1975. Here again I didn't get enough action to keep me busy.

I hadn't been totally convinced that Motown had seen the last of me. I could understand matters better if our music had stopped hitting, but that wasn't the case. The place just shut down.

The idea of uprooting my family and relocating to LA turned and twirled in my mind like a passing storm. It took some time to even mention this idea to my wife, Char. I didn't want her to think this was some vague or capricious idea that I hadn't given serious thought to. This would be a serious move – a challenge of success.

After hours and days of methodically planning and weighing possibilities I approached my wife with my proposal for relocating. She seemed to have realized the urgency of our situation and, without intense deliberation, we decided LA was in our future. Within a few weeks we had packed, sold the house (at a give-away price), and given our dog away.

That was really the most difficult part of the entire move. I had to give the dog away because the apartment that we were moving to didn't allow animals. Words are inadequate to describe the pain and hurt I endured as I released the leash to my dog's new master. I kissed and hugged him good-bye and told him how much I loved him for being the best dog I ever had. As they walked away, he stared into my eyes as though he really understood. I wasn't worried because I knew that he was with a new and caring owner. My heart burned with deep sadness as I held back the tears. I really loved my dog. He was a trophy-winning Doberman.

The day came when it was time to let go of all the thoughts of what Detroit once meant to me and 'Exit Stage Left'.

I was born in Philadelphia, but Detroit seemed more like home and I had millions of memories to pack away. It was a great twelve years, and now for LA our future home. We had planned the route with the same atlas that guided my way to Detroit. It would now guide us to LA. Actually I had mixed emotions about leaving, but 'A man's gotta do what a man's gotta do'. And so we did it. My wife, Char, My daughters Miko and Jakene. Oh! And Jakene's favorite stuffed animal 'Snoopy'. Miko was four years old and Jakene was about six months. So just a little after Christmas was over in 1975 we were en route to LA/Hollywood. The cross country drive in our blue Ford sedan went smoothly and without any incidents. The sights were so nice. It was hard to believe some of the breathtaking sceneries were not artificially contrived by man. Nature's hands had perfectly created beautiful backdrops for some wonderful snapshots of a few of the key points. Some of the cacti were tall as one storey buildings, and the surrounding mountains and mesas made the landscape complete and beautiful.

Around January 11, 1975, Char, the kids and I arrived in LA/ Hollywood, California..

This land was heavenly, but I could feel the vibes ushering me into a new way of life. The weather was hot. It was 90 degrees. It was difficult to believe that it was January.

After all, we had just left a ton of snow back east and now a few days later we were experiencing desert-like temperatures. The palm trees and vegetation thrived from the constant bearing down of the sun.

"Is this beautiful or what?" I asked. My wife loved it.

I suppose that I did too, but my focus was on music and I wanted to know when I could start working.

We checked into a hotel for a few days until our furniture arrived. The movers took a little longer than we did.

After we checked into a Hollywood hotel, Jamerson and Bongo rushed over to see us, and we all went to lunch. We had so much catching up to do until we hardly had time to eat. We acted like blood brothers who hadn't seen each other in years.

To tell you the truth, I don't think that we could have been closer. All during our relationship, we never argued or become angry. I'm speaking of my own personal relationship. With the Funks, we were 'straight up' with each other and very loyal. Bongo and Jamerson informed all of the producers that I was in California permanently ready to do sessions.

Passing the message on to producers and contractors began to pay off. Within just a couple of days the phone rang from a couple of producers and contractors.

If you guessed Ben Barrett, guess again. If Ben knew I was in town I'm sure he would have been somewhere muttering imprecations against me.

It was great people like McKinley Jackson that started calling me to work along with Arthur Wright, the arranger. Gene Page gave me a lot of action as well as his sister Olivia Page. My first session in LA was a Johnny Mathis session.

Ray Parker was right there plugging for me and helping to spread the news that I was a California resident. Ray's gesture was an outward display of acknowledging and respecting my inborn talent as a musician. He has always been one of my greatest fans and advocates.

My work had picked up tremendously. One by one the sessions came in and I was getting double and even triple scale pay. It felt good to once again be able to pay my bills and provide decently for my family. The flow of work was not comparable to the thriving sixties, but I wasn't borrowing to keep afloat.

I would always let Bongo know of any session overdubs and he would do the same for me. With certain receptive producers, I would remind them that Jamerson was still available too. In myself, I started to feel comfortable and halfway secure. I knew in order to sustain I had to remain vigilant and aggressive about securing session dates. In my greatest pursuits of work, I conducted myself in a way so that it wouldn't be said that I harried those in a position to call me for sessions. I just simply let my presence be known, and their fingers do the dialing. I never dismissed the facts regarding the reason why I had relocated to California and I didn't want the rug pulled from under me again.

I'm not one to wallow in the past, but the unforgettable 'shutdown' was still resting dormant in the corners of my mind.

Bongo was always combing the city, day or night, in an attempt to get on a session. It was a little more difficult for him because there were other bongo players who played well. Whereas those who could play the tambourine could not create with it and add that extra dimension to a track as I did.

I remember one night Jamerson, Bongo and I went out on the town and before retiring for the night we decided to run past the Motown studio where a session was in progress. We had seen Bobby Taylor earlier and he informed us of the action at the studio. Bobby Taylor was once a member of the Vancouvers and went on to become a producer. Bobby Taylor was the one who actually discovered the

Jackson Five. He knew the entire family in Indiana and brought them to Motown. The press was told that Diana Ross had discovered the group, but that was not the case.

Well, anyhow, when we all arrived at the studio a security guard was on duty screening all visitors.

He allowed Bongo and me to enter, but told Jamerson, "I have orders to keep you off the premises. You two guys can go on in, but Jamerson will have to leave."

I didn't believe what I was hearing. Now this is the same Jamerson that was the Motown genius and the greatest bass player that ever played on *any* Motown session.

This guard apparently didn't know his history and I thought that I would remind him of who he was talking to and barring out. "Did you know that this is James Jamerson, the all-time greatest bass player in the history of Motown?" I looked him squarely in the eyes and waited for an answer.

"Yeah, I know exactly who he is, and those are my orders, to deny him access to the studio at any time! What's so difficult to understand about that?"

Hearing these abrasive remarks of rejection, Jamerson showed outward signs of profound hurt and pain. Tears rolled down his face as he tried to explain he only wanted to visit the studio and wouldn't be a problem.

The security officer was really getting worked up and excited.

Bongo interrupted and said to Jamerson, "The same off limits treatment that applies to Jamerson will be applied to all Funk Brothers."

As a result of this, neither of us went in, and we left. We were all worn and tattered from the tribulations imposed upon us. It was twice as hard to understand the expelling of the Funks because there was no visible or audible reason.

You might wonder about some of the guys that held down the 'front office' in Motown's Detroit administrative office. They were left to wander and search through the ashes of Motown's once raging fire. These guys were ready to put their feet up on the coffee table of life and live happily ever after.

This was not the case, Berry acquired new players, and they suffered disappointments like the rest of us. Without naming names, and if you know anything at all about Motown, you know who these 'brown nosers' were.

I can say unequivocally that there were many studios in LA Sessions were going on around the clock, but never at any time did Bongo, Robert, Jamerson and I ever play on the same session. This was just a theory. What do you think?

NORMAN WHITFIELD AND I

Norman was one of those that followed Motown to its new Hollywood/LA address. He too had been victimized by the collapse of the company and had suffered a 'crash landing' down from 'Cloud Nine'. I worked with Norman on many, many, recording dates at the 'Snake Pit' and he always wanted me to play the tambourine. I played on songs like 'Cloud Nine', 'Papa was a Rolling Stone', 'War', 'Psychedelic Shack', and many more.

Norman's prodigious talent was phenomenal. He knew how to make a musician rock the tracks. While it's true he never attended a music school, a school of music could never teach students the way he put tracks together.

Norman hung around and tried to tough it out, but he had a very low tolerance level for abuse and didn't like the way he was being treated. He kissed Motown good-bye and launched his own company and named it – what other than Whitfield Records?

After venturing out on his own, he began recording and the hits started happening all over again with groups like Rose Royce, Star Guard and Junior Walker.

Rose Royce was probably the biggest act with their hits 'Wishing on a Star' and 'Car Wash'. Star Guard had a hit called 'Which Way Is Up?' Norman wrote the movie scores for both of the movies *Which Way Is Up?* and *Car Wash*. I'm sure that the music helped to sell both movies. Another one of his groups was The Undisputed Truth, whose hit was 'Smiling Faces'.

This group was once a Motown act but Norman bought the contract from Berry and signed them to his company. 'Smiling Faces' was their only hit.

Junior Walker, Spider Turner and Mammatapee never had any big hits.

I played on almost all of the tracks produced at Whitfield Records. Norman was cutting seven days a week usually because he had his own studio and if the senior engineer, Leonard Jackson, or Steve Smith wasn't available, Norman or his son, Norman Jr. could operate the board. Norman was busier than a one-armed paper hanger trying to write, produce, arrange and take care of the paperwork too.

The studio was located on Melrose Avenue, cuddled between two antique shops. The studio was not elaborate, but was tastefully done. Norman provided lots of food and games for session breaks. If you had to be detained, there was always something to keep you entertained and happy. Various writers and artists would come by the studio to practice, write, or record. The door was always open. Norman's brother Bill was the office manager as well as the studio manager.

The combination of duties and the fast pace of activities proved to be too much for Norman to handle. It was clear that the studio could not accommodate the need and acquiring an office space was imperative. There were a few available places on Melrose, but an upstairs corner property with a view put a look of approval on Norman's face and he immediately signed the lease.

Norman always had an eye for unusual decorative conversation pieces and did a fine job decorating the office which was located on the corner of Santa Monica and Westmoreland. The office was adorned with beautiful rugs, over-stuffed sofas, tropical plants, and the walls were partially garnished with gold and platinum records. It was very tastefully done.

Norman was aware that I had previous experience with my own company, and my expertise in music publishing would be an asset to him and his company. He approached me with his proposal about working for him, and I accepted. Also working in the office as secretaries, were his niece Pam, and Renea Featherstone. I was in charge of the publishing wing.

After spending a little time on the job organizing papers and files I made a major discovery regarding the publishing agreement between Norman and Warner Brothers. Without divulging the details I can say factually I saved Norman a ton of money. This incident seemed to have made my 'stock' go up. Norman now had a real appreciation for my music business aptitude, as well as for my talent as a musician.

He gave me high marks for possessing the ability to perform with remarkable versatility. He said to me so many times, "Jack you have enough balance to loan me some." That meant that I would do whatever was necessary to get the job done and still maintain a reasonable level of sanity. Our relationship grew closer and closer. I really asserted myself in Norman's company. I wanted more than anything to see his company flourish to its pinnacle of success. My unclouded rationale and diversified approaches were accepted as good looking out, or unwavering devotion to the company.

In many instances he would solicit my opinion before embarking upon a new task or adventures. Norman wanted to take every precaution necessary to build his company.

I can remember one night we went to a party that was attended by William Marshall, who played the lead role in *Blackula*, along with a relatively long list of the 'not so rich and famous' (and quite a few wannabes). The party was at some promoter's place, which was a swanky Beverly Hills mansion, decorated with elegance and refinement.

For a moment, I felt like I was amid the very wealthy and I lacked the status to be among those of greater means than my present position. The gracious host completed several rounds of introductions to the many overly made-up females and men pawning themselves as solid and successful businessmen.

They all stood around vocalizing many success stories that only existed in their minds. In other words, they were mostly lying about that enormous deal or big investment they claimed had materialized. It was like hearing a bunch of fishermen giving an account of the great number of fish caught and of course the big one that got away.

The final introduction and handshake went to an attorney who knew as much about music as an elephant knows about flying. At that time his law practice was not flourishing and he seemed to have been seeking refuge with Norman in an effort to recover. He was clinging to Norman throughout the evening expressing his reverence and admiration of Norman's talent.

I could smell a rat (no pun intended). His conversation never wavered from the task of convincing Norman that he was a notable attorney and eager to be a part of the company.

Norman turned to me for approval. "What do you think of him joining the company as General Manager?" As well as my rational perception served me, I felt he would just occupy space until we needed an attorney to go to court to settle a dog bite case.

I looked at Norman in disbelief and asked, "Does he know anymore now about the record and music business than he did fifteen minutes ago when he cornered you?"

Without saying anything, I could tell that he was wondering about what I had said and was searching for the right words. My disdainful attitude toward the attorney and the thought of having him as a part of the company was becoming obvious.

"Listen, Norman, he doesn't know the record business and he doesn't know entertainment law either. How can he become the general manager of your company?"

The attorney was too stunned by my abrasive remarks to comment. Imagine an attorney lost for words and looking rather sheepish. That should have sounded an alarm. Instead, Norman sensed that he had no defense and defended him by saying, "Oh, I'll teach him what he needs to know. I'll teach him".

Those words echoed through my ears like thunder. Suddenly, I had a brainstorm, and my mental tape recorder immediately shifted to reverse and played back an earlier incident of deception including an attempt to own all of Norman's copyrights without his knowledge. Was Norman the right guy to teach a 'greenhorn' like this the record business? I just shook my head and struggled to stay sane for the duration of the evening. I suspected that I would see the guy at Whitfield's as a part of the staff and BINGO!! I was correct.

He came on board, and of course you know already we didn't get along very well.

I was there to protect Norman's interest and anyone with another agenda was bound to collide with my efforts to do my job. He cost Norman a tremendous amount of money due to his legal limitations. Not only that, he was responsible for the loss of a valuable piece of real estate. It became obvious to everyone that he was nothing more than a 'glory hound'. It's too bad his motives didn't become apparent until thousands of dollars later. Day by day the company faded a little more due to leadership inadequacies.

Norman and I mutually appreciated each other's humor and wit. We had tons of fun together. considering neither one of us liked hanging around friends.

Our weekends were usually spent in Las Vegas. We called ourselves 'The Desert Dogs'. Drugs and alcohol had no place in our lives, so in our leisure time we would frequent that famous desert town. Norman had a great rapport with the 'pit boss' at the Aladdin and Caesar's Palace. We always had first class 'comps' whenever we went there.

There was no limit to the hospitality that 'Mr. W.' received. They treated him like a king. Of course since I was with him I got the 'King' treatment too.

There's one time that I still remember clearly. We were at Caesar's and bumped into Diana Ross. She was appearing there. Norman and Diana talked about the possibility of him producing her next album. Boy! That was quite exciting to me and I could see dollar signs in Norman's eyes. It was decided that they would meet the next day, same time and same place. Norman and I left Caesar's and made the tour of the casinos for the rest of the day and on into the next morning. The next day we went to breakfast and as the clock approached twelve noon, I reminded Norman of the meeting set with Diana Ross.

He looked at me and said "Man, forget that girl, I didn't really mean what I said."

I was shocked. I was dreaming of a future deal with Norman and Diana, and he told me that he didn't mean it. Their conversation was nothing more than 'mental masturbation'. It happens in the record business quite often. I had my selfish reasons of course for wanting this Whitfield/Ross production to be a reality. I could just visualize the huge role that I would play, but it was all talk, even from Diana.

It was common to bump into movie stars, recording artists, athletes, or anybody that was somebody, and Norman knew them all. We often saw Redd Foxx, Sammy Davis Jr, Berry Gordy, Gladys Knight, Leon Spinks, Ash Reisnick, Tony Bennett, and so many, many, more.

One night at the blackjack table, Martha Raye kissed me because I took a hit and gave her a chance to win. I was counting the cards. She won big money.

Norman's records were not scorching the charts as they once had. The impact of his failures affected me also. Music had made a transition and 'pulled the rug' right from under us with the disco sound and self-contained groups. The artists of the sixties had lost the intensity of their careers and found themselves 'wading in a sea of wonder' about their next move. Motown didn't have any great hits to speak of either. The artist roster was totally new, with the exception of Stevie Wonder and Smokey Robinson. Every artist that was once 'red-hot' now seemed to have cooled down and stood at some musical crossroad, wondering what to do next.

Norman and I spent countless hours listening to and dissecting the works of other producers in an effort to find out what made their hits a hit. Sometimes late at night we would meet at the office or have a telephone conference.

In California meetings were held at poolside, in the park, over lunch and several other places other than the typical office setting. Norman's favorite way to meet was the famous 'walking company meeting'. We would just stroll down Melrose Avenue that which adorned with quaint

124

little boutiques and antique shops. Occasionally, customers were seen darting to their cars with expensive purchases. The refreshing walks provided the needed privacy and made it easier to find solutions to perplexing business matters.

The Maumisaune Restaurant was on Melrose and Orson Welles had a table permanently reserved for himself and his friends there.

One day, while walking through the Hollywood streets, we found ourselves on Kings Road. Many occupants liked the royal implications of the street name as well as the scenic panoramic view it provided for one's optical pleasure. As we approached one of the buildings, Norman pointed out "Hey Jack, 'Blue' lives in this building. Let's see if he's home." ('Blue' was Melvin, the bass singer of the Temptations). We rang his doorbell and waited for an answer. I suppose since we 'popped up' unannounced, Melvin was trying to see who we were.

Just as we were about to leave, Melvin buzzed us in and we scurried up the steps to the second floor apartment. This was physically challenging since we were somewhat out of shape. Melvin's gladness at seeing us again was most touching. His euphoric behavior signaled that our visit had really made his day. We shook hands, embraced and Melvin insisted, "Come on in and take a seat in the living room." It wasn't difficult to overlook the fact that the coffee table was over-sized as well as the other items of furniture that decorated the small loft-type apartment. 'Back in the day', Melvin had lived in a mansion, but hard times had altered his lifestyle, and a small apartment suited his budget better.

Our conversation covered just about everything including the time Melvin was assaulted in Detroit. He elaborated on how a 'would-be-stick-up-man' jumped into his car brandishing a hand gun. Melvin explained:

"Man, this guy seemed to have been on drugs and was very offensive. He told me to give him my car keys all of my money. I hesitated and didn't move fast enough, so this dude fired the gun and the bullet hit me in the wrist and went on through and hit me in the leg. I pleaded to the robber, 'Please don't kill me, I'm Melvin with the Temptations.' He looked at me and said 'Oh my God, hey man I'm sorry. I didn't know who you were.'

"This guy threw the money on the seat and ran. I saw my life pass right in front of me. God saved me that time."

Melvin stated further that even though the incident happened a few years ago, he still felt the repercussions. We were really moved by

Melvin's story and agreed he was a blessed man to be able to talk about his experience and he was not a fatality.

During this time, around 1980, The Temptations were in between record deals and were not working steady at all. Tears in Melvin's eyes gathered silently as he expressed how family and friends hang around when there is plenty of money, but quickly become distant when your pockets are empty. He said it was difficult to be accused of not providing properly for his family. I really understood and felt his pain.

He walked to the window and said, "I feel like jumping out of this window and ending it all." Norman was visibly shaken and showed concerned by saying: "Trouble don't last always, and things are gonna get better."

I sat there trying to think of something to say that would lift his spirits a little because I really had the feeling Melvin couldn't continue in this frame of mind, especially, with Christmas approaching. No money plus Christmas right around the corner seemed to be the formula for encouraging deep depression and self destruction.

I thought about Paul Williams, a former Temptation, who took his own life early on back in Detroit when the group was hot on the charts. With every fiber in me, I wanted to be of some assistance.

"I got an idea, Norman, why don't you produce an album on the Temps? You once had them as the hottest R&B group in the world. I really think that it could work."

Just hearing those words obliterated the negative thoughts Melvin had moments earlier. He was ecstatic. He began prancing and declaring, "This could work, Norman, we can do it again, this could work man!"

Norman slowly replied, "Well, yeah, it could work, but I couldn't afford to put you guys on my label. See by the time I gave y'all advances and manufactured the records, I would be damn near broke." (Remember that Whitfield Records was distributed by Warner Brothers.)

I obstructed Norman's next words by saying, "Why don't I set up an appointment with Berry Gordy and sell him on the idea and let him run with the package?"

That sounded good to all three of us and we agreed to try it.

"First," Melvin explained, "You have to try to get Dennis (Edwards) in here from Cleveland, Ohio. He's working with a construction company operating a jack hammer."

"A jack hammer? Are you sure?" I asked. I couldn't believe what I was hearing. It was evident that the Temps were seriously out of the music loop and needed something or somebody to help them to recover. Melvin gave me Dennis's phone number and told me the best time to reach him. As we started to leave, Norman gave him a fist full of hundreds. Naturally, this made Melvin feel someone had appreciation and compassion for him. He was extremely grateful and saw the dim light at the end of the tunnel appear slightly brighter.

I could hardly wait to get back to the studio to call Dennis in Ohio. (This was before the cellular phone was popular.)

Much to my disappointment, Dennis didn't answer the phone and I had to leave a message. I assumed the arrangement we discussed with Melvin would also be agreeable with Dennis. So to expedite matters I called Berry's office and set an appointment with his secretary, Edna.

The following day Dennis returned my call. I explained what we had planned and he was very receptive and excited about the entire deal. Dennis declared, "It's been my fervent prayer for God to provide me with something so I could get back into the music business and quit this construction job. When do I come?"

He asked that question before I could even answer. I assured him that it would be very soon, and within a week we met Dennis at LAX Airport. He was 'hyped up' and acted like this was his first time away from home as a new artist.

All the way from the airport Dennis cranked out song after song as though he was doing a self imposed audition, or maybe he was trying to assure me that he 'still had it'.

We went to the studio and then dinner at a first class restaurant. Afterwards, we checked him into a hotel. Norman gave him the 'star' treatment. Personally, I admired Norman for the nice gestures, because he really wasn't obligated to do that.

Melvin and Dennis were informed of the date of the meeting with Berry. On the day of our appointment we drove down Sunset Boulevard to the Mowest office at 6464 Sunset Boulevard.

On the way I casually said to Norman, "I hope Melvin isn't late because I want Berry to know that we are serious."

Norman agreed and reminded me, "This could be something great for everybody. I would be happy with another shot at producing the Temps, W-O-O-O-O!"

When we arrived at the Mowest office, we were greeted by Edna.

Elegance embraced every inch of the office. She escorted us to the conference room and we were seated at this long conference table that accommodated about twelve people. The table glistened as though its highly polished surface was wet. The plush leather burgundy chairs seemed to announce 'Success dwells in these cushions'. All of the furnishings throughout the Gordy establishment were classy and well selected.

Edna offered us beverages from the bar or a cup of coffee. We were too anxious to even sip a swallow of water. I checked my watch continuously. The clock was getting closer and closer to our appointment but Melvin hadn't arrived.

I remembered that Melvin had made the comment that he wanted a $50,000 advance for each member of the group upon signing. So I figured a man with that kind of expectation of money would likely be on time. I certainly would have, had it been me.

We sat a few more minutes and the clock struck one p.m., which was the time of our appointment.

Without warning, one of the walls of the conference room opened. It revealed Berry and he walked right over to where we were.

"How dramatic was that?" I said "Well, Berry, you are still doing things in grand style." We all had a big laugh as we shook hands and exchanged expressions of smalltalk like "How have you been? What's going on?", etc.

I was attempting to act as though I wasn't concerned about the absence of Melvin, but I had begun to worry. The conversation broke away suddenly from the BS and Berry spoke directly to the point without showing any signs of remorse or regret and said, "I know that you guys are here to meet with me about the Temps, but Melvin was here yesterday, and we were able to cut a nice deal."

Norman and I both were stony-eyed and speechless for a moment.

To avoid saying something negative, I blurted out, "Oh yeah?"

Norman was disappointed, but he took the news well. Berry tried to assure him that he had a better deal for him to produce some other act in the company. Norman's reply was, "I'll get back with you in a couple of days."

Out of courtesy we all shook hands again and made our exit through Berry's private corridor. I knew Norman well enough to know that "I'll get back to you later" translated to "Go to hell" or maybe something worse. We drove back to the office in total disbelief that Melvin had back-doored us and never bothered to call.

Plus, he allowed us to go to Berry's office to be humiliated. How ungrateful! Now what kind of s--- was that? Melvin did the same thing that Berry did when he moved the company from Detroit to LA. Melvin never called, and he never acknowledged that Norman and I were responsible for 'pulling The Temptations' nuts out of the fire'. I should have been very angry, but I felt good about the fact that through our efforts we were actually the ones that were responsible for raising the Temps from the dead, so life could be pumped into them again. No one would touch them when their careers fell upon hard times.

Just remember you know the real true story of the Temptations' rebirth into the music industry. To this day, they have never said thanks – not ever.

We recovered from that escapade and proceeded on with our own artists. We still had Rose Royce, Junior Walker, Mammatappie, Willie Hutch, The Undisputed Truth and a couple of other acts.

Norman had recorded several tunes on the acts. Some were released and some were canned.

The relationship with Warner Brothers and Whitfield Records collapsed leaving me to wonder again about my financial future.

Another crossroads and more turbulence, somewhere in life I must have offended the Gods of music. My self confidence and patience were being tested again. I didn't like it, but what could I do? I was the architect of my dreams, so it was back to the drawing board.

Norman was now faced with reducing the staff to the bare minimum which included only his brother Bill, a secretary and me. Cash flow was very necessary to avoid a shut down. My salary had been slashed, but I never lagged with my efforts to help. The laborious job ahead to keep the company afloat was as difficult as a soldier digging twenty new fox holes overnight.

My loyalty to Norman motivated me to create something sensational. Once more, Norman and I took one of our famous 'think tank' walks to attempt to think of something to alter the downward spiraling of the company. We tossed around several possibilities, but one seemed more profitable than anything else.

I suggested we acquire a loan from Warner-Tamalane Music Publishing Company. Norman didn't think that it would work because of the previous incident he had with Ed Silvers that almost ended with an exchange of blows. Nobody applauded Norman for losing his temper, but they did know that Norman was a great producer with a proven record. I finally convinced Norman that it could really work – only if he stayed away from the meeting.

My strategy froze him in his tracks. My plan was to ask for $300,000. He stared at me with a perplexed look and said: "OK, let me get this right. You're going to ask for $300,000, and I should stay home. Pull this off and your commission is $10,000"

That naturally raised my interest to a different level. I made the appointment and rehearsed my presentation. Within a couple of days I was sitting in Chuck Kay's office explaining my plan. He was very receptive and okayed the deal. In a few days Norman got the check and I got the bonus.

Norman just couldn't believe that I had pulled this deal off. The money helped everybody. We all let out a sigh of relief. I shared my blessing with Eddie Bongo.

It had been a long time since he had a session, so what I gave him was well needed.

The money kept the studio open for a while. Norman produced a few tunes on Junior Walker but the tunes were never released.

The nation loved the records Norman created in the past, but the magic the company once had just wasn't there anymore. The company's future was uncertain and the unfortunate circumstances fate had chosen for the Whitfield dynasty were enough to sink it.

We gave it our best shot but the inevitable took over, and like the great *Titanic* we went down. That was a tragedy.

ANOTHER VEGAS VENTURE

Norman and I went to Vegas frequently. This particular weekday evening, Norman walked into my office near closing time with the look of 'Let's hit the road' twinkling in his eyes. "Lock up and let's get out of here," Norman insisted. I had a few more things to do and then we did it. This was during the time when there was a gas shortage and if you were planning to travel it was necessary to seriously plan your traveling times. We got on the interstate highway and began heading for Vegas.

The vehicle we were traveling in was a beautiful brand new Jensen. I glanced at the gas hand and reminded him that we were getting low on gasoline.

"Shouldn't we purchase gasoline before we leave the LA area?" I asked.

He totally disagreed with me. "We have *plenty* of gas and we can get gas on the way down there," Norman explained. I could plainly see that the gasoline hand was closer to 'E' than any of the other indicators. I knew that unless this car with its aluminum engine ran off of air, we were in for a long night, parked a long way from Las Vegas. My gut feeling became the sickening truth as the car began to sputter and miss. We coasted into a gas station that was closed in Victorville, California. This was less than an hour from LA.

We had to spend the entire night there in the car, sitting in front of a gas pump. The only advantage to that was we would be the first in line the next morning. I wanted to say I told you so, but Norman's actions made it unnecessary. We became chilled with the declining night's temperature. We couldn't start the engine to turn on the heater because we had an empty gas tank. So we froze. The next morning as the sun was just peeping from behind the mountains, the station opened for business. We were two happy guys. We got a full tank of gas and proceeded on to Vegas. This was insane, but that's how we operated.

Another encounter of the 'Desert Dogs' (Norman and me) was when we were in Vegas and really hadn't been there but a few hours before becoming almost broke. It was mid-February and we were wearing only lightweight clothing because it wasn't very cold there. In an effort to get more gambling money, Norman called BMI in New York. He told the representative that he wanted a $15,000 advance.

With Norman being a successful writer, he had plenty of money in reserve. The advance was OK'd and the person on the phone instructed Norman that she would put the check in the mail.

He informed her, that he would be on the next flight from Vegas and pick the check up in person. I was flabbergasted and so was the representative. I'm sure there weren't too many people that did business in this manner. What drama! I told Norman that I would remain in Vegas until he got back.

But of course, you know he bought a one way plane ticket for both of us to New York.

The ride there was quite lengthy and we slept much of the way. When we arrived, people of all nationalities were walking around with coats, scarves and gloves because it was cold. We looked like two guys on the run with only shirts and sweaters on buffing the freezing temperatures. The wind from the Hudson River was bone chilling and I thought I just couldn't continue without a coat. Norman assured me that he would buy coats after we picked up the $15,000.

We went directly to BMI and everyone was nice until they discovered that he didn't have his wallet. No wallet, no ID, no way to get the check. He could have been anybody as far as BMI knew. They knew the name but not the face. Picture this. Two guys in New York, who traveled on a one way ticket there, improperly dressed, and trying to pick up a big check without identification. What could have been worse?

After several calls were made, they finally found the lady that Norman called from Vegas and they released the check. We left BMI and went to the bank and immediately Norman was met with opposition in his efforts to cash the check without identification and no way of proving who he was. Actually, I thought maybe he would be arrested attempting to conduct such business without the proper credentials. This seemed to have aroused everybody's suspicions. The teller talked to several others at the bank and they began to whisper and look over at us with questioning looks.

Norman said: "All you have to do is call BMI. They'll tell you who I am, they know me over there." Eyebrows were raised and Norman was given an earful as the teller informed him she would not call BMI to verify the check, nor to verify who he was. She said that was not a part of her job description. So Norman had to get on the phone and call BMI and have them call the bank and verify who he was, and to give the OK to cash the check.

Finally, the check was cleared and Norman had money – $15,000 all in one hundred dollar bills, which were stuffed in his pockets and made him look as though he was carrying lunch.

Before doing anything else I reminded him that we needed to buy coats and gloves. The first store we saw we bought coats. We didn't secure a return flight to Vegas that night but instead we had to get a hotel room for an overnight stay. We went to Gallagher's Restaurant and feasted on an enormous size steak. These steaks were some of the biggest steaks I've ever seen. It was like having a side of beef on my plate.

While we were eating, in walks an attorney that Norman knew. She was there to negotiate the sale of the Aladdin Hotel and Casino. She had dinner with us and our conversation was lengthy because we knew as much about the Aladdin as she did. We knew everybody that she knew. After resting overnight in a very swanky hotel, we took a flight back to Vegas where Norman was given a luxury suite at the Aladdin. We went back to the dice table and the 'party was on' again. We gambled non-stop, until it was time to go back to LA to work.

EARL'S HOME GOING

The news of Earl's death in 1992 was painful and difficult to bear. It was like a bullet tearing out my heart. How could this be? Life seemed so short for him in spite of the fact that he had lived far past a half century. I had been to see Earl during his illness, but I couldn't come to grips with the fact that he was terminally ill.

When Earl passed away I was living in Memphis, Tennessee, practically buried in my own shortcomings, and far away from any trace of music business. Stax had been long gone, and any other efforts to rekindle The Memphis Sound was a job for Superman.

The day Earl expired, I was actually in Atlanta, Georgia, networking trying to get something going musically. My wife called and told me. Since I was living in a foreign country (the south) I immediately called one of the Funk Brothers or someone I felt akin to. As I phoned for confirmation I prayed: "Please God, don't let this be true."

But it was true. Earl was gone.

For several years, Earl had played with signature musicians on sessions at Motown, on tours, at Stax, United Sounds, for HDH, in night clubs and many other places.

He was the powerful magnetic force that kept the Funks focused. We owed him so much for his leadership, loyalty, competence, and his caring ways. Earl was plucked from his earthly vivacious existence to relocate on a heavenly plane.

Eddie Willis (guitarist and Funk brother) lived about ninety miles south of Memphis, in Grenada, Mississippi. We both wanted to attend the funeral so we decided that we would drive to Detroit by way of Nashville to pick up Bob Babbitt (bass player).

Nashville and Memphis are separated by just two hundred miles. I hadn't seen Bob in over ten years. I was quite elated to see him, but regretted the circumstances that united us. We must have embraced and slapped backs for more than ten minutes. Of course, much of the same happened with Bob and Eddie.

As soon as we were back on the Interstate, we were deeply engaged in conversations about the past. Eddie was driving and in no time we were crossing the Tennessee state line and on into Virginia. Neither the winding highway that had almost ninety degree turns, nor the altitude of the Smokey Mountains, bore any significance. We were swallowed up with reminiscing about Motown and how we loved Earl.

Eddie never stopped unless the gas hand was approaching empty. He made it clear that the trip was not a pleasure trip, so therefore he would only be stopping for gasoline. Our conversation never ceased, there was so much to talk about.

Sooner than I had ever imagined, the road mileage signs were showing Detroit only a hundred miles away, fifty miles away and then 'Detroit city limits'. Well, we were in Detroit, but the reality of why we were there weakened our conversation, and our laughter ceased.

The city hadn't changed much. The skyline had a couple of changes with the casinos in town and Motown was now a museum. We made our way through town to a motel that Allen Slutsky had reserved for us. We met Allen there and checked in.

The next day we drove to the church where the funeral was held. We took a seat in the rear of St Mary's Catholic Church, and waited for Earl's funeral service to commence. I was flanked by Eddie Willis and Bob Babbit. The church was completely filled from front to back except for the few rows draped in black and marked reserved for the family. There wasn't a whisper nor a word uttered from anyone. The mood of grief and sadness blanketed the sanctuary.

Familiar faces dotted the church pews here and there. I just nodded to a few of those that I knew. I walked down the aisle to the closed casket that was draped across the altar.

I felt my heart pounding, and my throat swelling as I touched his picture to bid farewell.

"Take your rest, my brother Earl. You will sure be missed. You're taking a chunk of the funk with you." The tears blurred my vision and rolled from under my glasses.

I blotted the tears as I found my way back to the rear of the church. Even the tall gray church pillars seemed to cry out and express their woe right along with those attending.

There was no solace. His steel-gray casket solemnly bore the United States flag and the beautiful wreaths permeated the room with the smell of roses.

The playing of soft organ music encouraged my mind to reflect on some of the wonderful times that Earl and I shared together as friends, as musicians and as brothers. I fondly remembered the times when I first relocated to Detroit and he and his wife Doris would baby sit for Earline and me. (Earline was my lady at the time.) He would tell me to bring the

135

kid over any time. They were so nice about things like that. He was like a big brother to me – a few years older with plenty of advice, whether I asked for it or not.

During that first rehearsal at Motown with Marvin Gaye, we auditioned and, without knowing, I was doing an audition on vibes for Earl as well. After everything was over that day, he introduced himself, and "Man, I really like the way you jam on those vibes. I'll be working at the Chit Chat Lounge tonight. Why don't you come over and play with us tonight as a guest musician?"

This fast paced chain of events was like a lightning bolt striking me and I needed a 'shock absorber'. Except for being overwhelmed, I didn't really have a reason to reject the offer, but I blurted out, "I can't make it tonight, but how about next weekend?"

Earl agreed and it was a date. My first night at the Chit Chat was aired live on the Radio and recorded. After that night Earl said, "I want you on the payroll."

From that night on, I was a member of his band. The club was always crowded when we played. Half of Motown would be there when they were in town between gigs.

Earl was a wise ol' owl and was very organized. Before his death he had fortified Doris with any necessary details to make his transition occur smoothly, without difficulty.

The Funk Brothers really didn't have a designated leader but Earl projected that image and everyone made that assumption.

I was ushered back to the present moment when I heard the priest say, "All rise please." Everyone stood as he slowly led the procession down the aisle reading the twenty-third psalm and other scriptures. The pall bearers were just in front of Doris, who led a host of family members that filed by Earl's casket.

A cloud of sorrow hovered the entire church. There wasn't a dry eye in the building, and you could hear people quietly sobbing. I struggled with the reality of what today really meant. Earl's work is complete and he leaves us now, to unfurl his talents in high places.

Uriel Jones, Allen Slutsky, and an organ player (I don't remember who) played some of Earl's favorite tunes.

The entire service was tastefully done, and I think Earl would have approved of how he was eulogized. Knowing Earl as I did, I wouldn't be surprised if he had made it known to Doris how he wanted the service conducted. He was just that kind of guy.

When the priest ended his timely eulogy and called for the morticians, that was a signal that the service ended. The priest led the procession with the pall bearers following closely. This time Earl's casket was followed by the family.

As the casket was pushed out slowly, I touched it as a final gesture of my love and respect for this great legend. Friends in attendance followed the family and soon the church was devoid of its mourners.

The media, both TV and newspaper personnel combed the premises for any celebrities. I made my way over to the funeral car where Doris was. I barely got through the host of people wanting to express their sympathy also. We clung to each other as we embraced.

My grief and compassion was almost reduced to silence. I managed to blunder the words, "I'm sorry, and I'll miss him." Doris knew, beneath my dark shades and rehearsed smile, I was a broken hearted Funk Brother.

I spotted Stevie Wonder in the crowd. We embraced and expressed how glad we were to 'see' each other.

I expected more people from Motown, but Stevie was the only one there other than the Funks. Pistol Allen, Uriel Jones, Bob Babbitt, Joe Hunter, Eddie Willis, and Beans Bowles (a musician and close friend of the Funks) all attended.

As the crowd mixed and intermingled outside, the musicians stood on the church steps and continued to play. What a great send off!

The Funks stood around, chatted, and reminisced about some of our past experiences. We soon parted, but did not go to the cemetery.

The eventful life of Earl Van Dyke, was en route to its final resting place. His resounding traits and legacy will forever live in our hearts.

Rest In Peace, Earl.

MARVIN GAYE

Marvin Gaye was the real reason that I was at Motown. There's no way I would have ever considered giving up jazz to play the kind of music Motown produced if it hadn't been for him. I felt close to him because he was responsible for the major changes in my life that led me to a new beginning. The fate that befell me was not just by chance, but was a spiritual elevation that allowed me to levitate to unimaginable prominence in the world of music. I reflect and wonder what would have happened to me if I hadn't gone to work that night Marvin stopped at the club in Boston. Would I still be in Boston, or in my home town Philadelphia? I can only believe this was one of God's supernatural interventions upon my life. When you pray a supernatural prayer, take it from me, you'll get supernatural results. Marvin was a God-fearing man and was not ashamed to talk about his Christian beliefs. No matter what he did, he believed that God was the driving force in his life.

Marvin and I had a common interest. He thought that I was a pretty talented guy who wrote the kind of ballads that he liked. Marvin's hidden desire was to become a 'balladeer'. He composed and recorded a few songs of that genre, but they never made the charts. He wanted to sing some of my songs, but it meant that I would lose ownership of all publishing rights. I refused the deal.

We had actually gone into the studio and recorded one of my songs entitled 'Now She's Gone'. I was made aware of the publishing arrangements and that killed the completion of the song.

I must say that was a beautiful ballad and Marvin loved it. He had poured his heart into the song and shared my disappointment, but he wasn't the decision maker.

Who knows? In spite of the song being good it may have gotten buried like 'When I'm Alone I Cry'. That was an album of ballads beautifully done by Marvin, but went nowhere fast.

Sometimes when we were in the studio at the end of a session, Marvin would play beautiful ballads on the piano, even 'Now She's Gone'. He respected my talent, and had a special love for the tambourine. He would often pick it up and try to imitate me. He wasn't bad at all. Remember, Marvin had a strong church background and they used the tambourine in the church service. He would say things like, "How do you make this tambourine sing?" or "Why can't I make this thing sound the same as when you're playing it?" He said he would never forget playing the tambourine in his dad's church, and he loved the 'flavor' it added to the track.

Marvin's love for jazz often surfaced. On live shows he would have me push my vibes to the front of the stage where he would sit on a stool, have the lights dimmed, and would sing a few ballads or jazz tunes. This naturally was a variation from the show plan, but Marvin just wanted to do this. The audiences didn't appreciate the ballads as much as 'What's Going On', or some other up-tempo tune. After Marvin sung to fulfill his own personal enjoyment, he would get right back to what the audience wanted. He was a smooth performer and always left the audience wanting more.

Now and then, we would just sit, talk, and reminisce. He always wanted me to mentally glance at the past and entertain him with my experiences as a jazz musician. He never failed to encourage me to somehow arrange for my songs to be recorded. I really felt honored by his endorsement.

Marvin called me once in the middle of the night to do an overdub. Right away I could hear excitement bubbling in his voice. A genius was at work. "I'm at the studio. Get here as soon as you can, and bring your bags of tricks. I need you to make this thing come alive. This one's a hit, and you're gonna love it!"

Truer words were never spoken. The song was 'Got To Give It Up'. This was indeed a real hit. I, along with several other million people, loved it.

I invented a new instrument called the 'Hotel Sheet'. (It was nothing more than a measured piece of styrene that I found in a shipping crate. I held it a certain way and it made a musical sound). I told Marvin about the 'Hotel Sheet'.

"Let's see what it sounds like on tape." I played it on 'Got To Give It Up' and he liked it. He questioned why I called it the 'Hotel Sheet', but thought it was a unique item. He held it and as usual he played it. He declared, "Jack, nobody on the planet Earth can play your stuff like you!"

He gave me label credits for percussion – and the credits also read, "Jack Ashford on the Hotel Sheet." After the record had been released, he told me that people had started asking him what the hotel sheet was. He had someone to take pictures of him and me holding the 'Hotel Sheet'. That same picture has appeared in several magazines, and been seen all over the world. (This picture also served as a product endorsement).

I remember near the end of Marvin's life he called me and explained that he was thinking of planning a Russian tour. He wanted to know if I would be interested in joining him. I told him to contact me when he made some definite plans and if it did manifest, I would go with him. I didn't know if he was still getting high, but I was curious. There was a time that Marvin sometimes imagined that he was being trailed by the CIA, and a few other bizarre things.

So yes, I wasn't sure Marvin was really real and I had some reservations about getting excited and starting packing. There's one thing I did know. If the tour had come about, it would have really been wonderful. Marvin still had his golden voice and anywhere he performed, he would have been as captivating as ever.

When Marvin died, it was like he was a member of everybody's family. Fans all over the world were sobbing openly, and found themselves in a state of disbelief. The inner walls of my soul were flooded with intense pain and sadness.

It was April 1, 1983 and I was living in Memphis, Tennessee. On that particular day, I was on my way home with the radio on. The DJ announced "Marvin Gaye is dead!" It was April Fool's Day, and I assumed that it was his distasteful way of telling an April Fool's Joke.

"This is not a joke," he assured the listeners. He continued several times "This is not a joke, it's really true. Marvin Gaye is dead and was shot by his father."

I pulled over to the shoulder of the expressway to just gather my thoughts and try to make some sense of what I had heard. I was familiar, very familiar, with the social side of Marvin's character, but I never got involved with his family matters. The family things that I was aware of were either things that I read or someone told me. I couldn't think of any reason why anyone would end Marvin's life, especially his father. It was not for me to understand. This 'Troubled Man' with his frequently imitated sexy moves, talent and style, had now become history. I didn't want to accept it then and I don't want to accept it now.

MARVIN GAYE

I often listen to Marvin's music and wonder what would have happened if Marvin had lived. Sometimes when I play back my mental tape recorder I can hear and see him very vividly like it was yesterday and we were in the studio or on tour. 'Ain't Nothing Like The Real Thing'. There will never be another Marvin Gaye.

AFTER EARL'S FUNERAL

Allen Slutsky had arranged for the Funk Brothers to assemble at Uriel Jones's mother's house for filming. Just the thought of the Funks being filmed, and the spotlight turned on us was a little unbelievable. I kept wanting to ask Allen if he was sure, or would some star take center stage instead of The Funk Brothers.

This was just too unbelievable. I was excited, but my heart was still weighing heavy from the death of Earl. The drive to the house was filled with befogged anticipation. I could feel the anxiety mounting minute by minute.

We finally arrived and were warmly welcomed as though we were biological family members being united once again. The fine cherry dining room table was massive in size and comfortably accommodated all of us, as we reminisced about Earl and other highlights of our Motown careers. I became preoccupied with the thought that 'these moments are actually being recorded. This is priceless'.

We relived many of the experiences we had with Earl, and how he was regarded as our leader. The truth is we really didn't have a leader. Let's say Earl was the leader of the gig that we worked at night – that transcended right on into the studio where he would suggest a lot of things. And something else – when a producer came to the studio, he would go to the piano first to show the musicians what was needed. So therefore, the producer would be sitting right there with Earl, so he could be getting with Earl on what he wanted and Earl would then say. "OK, this is what you want?"

When the producer would say, "yeah,"' Earl would say something like "OK. Jack, I'm voicing this chord this way," or "Robert, I'm voicing this chord this way." So for all intents and purposes for somebody looking at it, it would seem that Earl was the leader.

Earl had a way with his eyes that transmitted discreet messages that only the Funks could perceive the meaning of.

Beans Bowles spoke up and pointed out what crowned our success. "You guys had great eye contact."

I couldn't argue that point. We always looked at Earl as he directed us with his head, and sometimes we would just stare at him and the message seemed to just instinctively transmit.

Our rhythm was so tight and synchronized that most groups would need a click track to keep the rhythm as solid as ours was. The only thing we needed was each other.

How did the Funks keep such tight rhythm? That was a fiery question everybody would always ask. Our only explanation was that we provided a natural marriage for each other's talent, and we were spiritually connected.

"These guys loved each other and even had fun talking about each other's mamas. They made history and were great stars only known to Berry Gordy" Beans sadly expressed.

Uriel used his cup as a gavel to get everybody's attention to what he had to say. "Motown at its peak could take an artist if he could sing just a little bit, put him in Motown's studio, and they could come up with a hit with the Motown sound," Uriel explained.

I concurred by saying, "Norman Whitfield once said you could bring a chicken to the studio, squeeze his neck, make him squawk on two and four, and you had a hit record." The house rocked and rolled with laughter on that one.

Those statements were funny, but they were very true. The truth is, we had the formula for getting hit records. Even if the Funk Brothers' faces could not be identified, or their names known, millions rocked to our rhythm.

We couldn't talk about anything without mentioning Earl's name. I recalled, "I remember when the session was on the line, we depended on Earl's expertise and knowledge to keep everything together. When we did that song 'Oooh Baby, Baby', they took my vibes and put them in the middle of the studio, right in the middle of two mikes. I was looking at Earl and I was playing the vibe figure in a single octave. I read Earl's look like a news flash. No one saw him signal me to play correctly (sending private messages without speaking was his specialty), but anyway, I immediately changed on the second measure, and played it in two octaves.

If you listen carefully to the record, you can actually hear the change. Earl's special way of communicating was probably the key to his cohesiveness with us.

"Hey what about Stevie? I said. "Man, y'all remember when he always wanted to hang out with us? We couldn't get rid of this guy. Stevie was in school with us but never said it. He was learning everything he could. He literally picked our brains.

Stevie was one of the few from Motown that attended Earl's funeral.

One of the TV media stations interviewed Stevie, and he referred to Earl as the foundation of Motown. "He taught me how to play the piano," said Stevie.

Everybody had a story to tell, and it appeared that Pistol was about to burst. "Bennie Benjamin taught me to play drums the Motown way. I used to listen to Spike Jones, Buddy Rich and other drummers, but Bennie was the one that created that famous Motown beat. "I tried to play as good as he did. He taught me the fundamentals. I was a jazz musician, and at that time if you didn't fit in, out cha would go. I caught hell, I really had to listen and learn."

As Pistol further explained, "Each drummer had a distinctive sound." He demonstrated by hitting the table, sounding out Bennie's beats, his beats and Uriel's beats. He was absolutely right, because each drummer had their own distinctive drum beats. Pistol's demonstration was very clear.

I thought to myself what a great way to relive those unforgettable times. We should have done this sooner. I can imagine how Jesus felt at the last supper – sitting around the table, talking, and sharing with his most trusted servants.

The camera rolled on as Eddie Willis revealed the true method or 'expert way', Junior Walker's 'Shotgun' was recorded.

He said, "We all went to the studio, tuned up, and was ready to play. "Just as we were given the signal to start playing, someone accidentally hit the amplifier and it made a loud shattering sound with the reverberation. That sound became the intro to 'Shotgun'.

With Eddie recalling the 'accidental genius' of the kicked over amp, I had to remind the gang how the sounds were made on 'Baby Love'.

"We actually cut the tune, and got it on tape. Brian Holland then laid planks on the studio floor and miked them. They were actual planks – the only thing missing was the nails. These were some serious planks right off the back fence. I had never seen anything like it!

"I thought that it was simply incredible. Brian would instruct everybody just where to put their feet. He would say things like, 'Put your foot up a little closer.' So if you had a pair of bad shoes with a hole in one of 'em, that would give two pitches.

"You would have to leave because you were wearing two-pitched shoes." The laughter roared throughout the house.

As soon as the laughter died down a little, Bob Babbitt gave accolades to the genius of James Jamerson: "Nobody played his style. After listening to Jamerson, it was hard to listen to anybody else. On 'Bernadette' and 'Reach Out', it was like he just had something within and he had to let it out," said Babbitt. "The sound was tremendous! I don't know if it was the studio, the bass, the touch, or the combination, but it was hard to listen to Jamerson's playing, and accept any other bass player's style. He had a special feel for his instrument," Babbitt recalled.

Robert White (guitarist) was another one of our fallen comrades. His famous licks on 'My Girl' are familiar and loved by several generations.

He really should have been here. He was told that he had clogged arteries. Robert discussed the problem with a friend and fellow guitarist from Motown, who lived in LA. Robert had some reservations about the surgical process, but took his friend's advice and decided to follow through with the surgery.

It was appalling. The hospital and the doctors were far from being the best. They did a 'botched' job.

Due to stupid and careless mistakes, Robert fell into a coma for about a week or so.

Allen Slutsky made several recordings of the Funks talking which were played for him. He responded to our voices, but it just wasn't enough. Robert slipped deeper and deeper, then finally the inevitable, he passed away on August 27, 1994.

I don't have to say that the friend that suggested the surgery to Robert was totally devastated. It really saddened him to know that Robert had followed his advice and was now gone from this earth.

Robert's death created an immense void in our lives. We never expected anything like this. After all, thousands have the surgery and live healthy lives afterwards. Reviewing Robert's tragedy triggered my mind to speculate about some 'What ifs'.

What if the Funks had an opportunity to prepare for the Motown shut down? What if we had gotten more work on the West Coast? What if the Funks had been given some kind of pension? Maybe if at least one of these had been in place, I firmly believe that Robert would have been given a fair chance to live life a little longer.

Deep down inside I realize my thoughts about this situation are nothing more than foiled frustration speaking. I must believe that Robert's destiny was appointed by God and he's with us right here...right now.

As the laughing and the talking continued, we began to focus on 'Mr. Funnyman' himself, 'Bongo Eddie'. Joe Hunter gave him that name. Just about everybody called Eddie Brown Bongo, but Joe Hunter called him Bongo Eddie.

I remember Eddie as a witty and a very compassionate person. Joking and making fun of people came very natural to him. He could imitate anybody, or come up with a funny line instantly. Eddie was the studio 'King of Comedy and the Dozens'.

James Jamerson was Eddie's favorite target for the 'dozens'. (The dozens was made up jokes about someone else's mama.)

Eddie back-doored his way into Motown as Marvin Gaye's valet. While its true Eddie eased his way in, his talent on the bongos and congas was phenomenal.. He became sought after by many producers. His voice was immortalized on the intro part of Marvin Gaye's *What's Going On?* album. That was Bongo doing most of the talking.

Likely we would have been there all night if Bongo had been there. Babbitt jokingly said "I'm a little different," (meaning he was the only white guy present), but made it clear he was never treated differently. "I just felt like a brother and a human being. We shared common interest – we wanted to play music."

The humor of the Funks got us through many tough times and helped us to release our stress. Those were fun times.

Sometimes it seemed like putting on a comedy show. If any of us lost our talent as a musician, we could have survived as a comedian.

STRUGGLING TO STAY AFLOAT

After Whitfield Records, I had nothing to depend on but a few session dates around LA. Some of the sessions were union and some were 'scabs'. It wasn't a lot of money but it was enough to pay the mortgage and buy a little food for my family. Eddie Bongo and I would share any knowledge of existing sessions going on. Sometimes if Eddie heard of a session he would load his drums into his car and go to it like he had been called. If by chance he did get hired, he would tell the producer that I was available too. We were actually begging for work, trying to make enough money to keep the lights on and a little food on the table. It was tough.

My life turned dark and gloomy in 1981. Studio musicians were suffering more now than ever. If I got one session per month it was almost like a miracle. The mortgage wasn't being paid on time and other bills had to be put on the back burner. A family insurance plan was a thing of the past.

Eddie Bongo got lucky when Liza Minnelli called him to go on the road to travel with her band. He took the gig and was making good steady money. He seemed to have been recovering from a long stretch without money. He was very glad and I was happy for him. Just as he was about to settle in and really enjoy being employed, his job was terminated by illness – his own illness.

Liza's road manager called and told me that he was sick and asked me to meet Eddie at the airport. I met him at LAX. I could readily see that he was profoundly ill. He appeared to be weak and his skin and eyes were yellow. I knew that the discoloration indicated jaundice. The urgency of his condition required immediate medical attention.

I wasted no time getting him to the hospital. We went directly to the hospital from the airport. He was admitted and treatment began right away.

His condition was contagious and he had to be isolated. I called him daily to make sure he was all right. Sticking by him was nothing new for the Funks. We always supported each other. I loved Eddie. He was my brother – my Funk Brother.

There was a time when Jamerson was in the hospital and Bongo was there for him. In fact Bongo was with Jamerson a few days before he died. Without reservation, we did whatever we could for each other. Our money was limited, but we shared sometimes our last.

We seemed to have taken turns attracting disastrous situations. This time it was my turn. My luck had turned bleak and I didn't seem to be able to get many prayers answered. I was not in the midst of a dream, this was reality with a capital R. On this dark day, I went jogging in the foothills of the Sierra Madre Mountains. (We lived in Pasadena, California where the Rose Bowl Parade traveled each New Year's Day.) After a great vigorous jog, I took a piping hot shower. Just as I was stepping out of the shower, I slipped and fell. On the way down, my elbow hit the glass door, broke it, and sliced my left arm wide open.

This was trauma in the worst way. I lost a lot of blood and I almost lost my arm. The cut was about six or seven inches long and very deep.

My wife Char was so alarmed she almost fainted. In fact I had to call 911 myself. Flowers and cards flooded my hospital room. Even Norman sent a big floral arrangement.

The doctors were very concerned at first that I might be in danger of infection or even worse. I could have lost my arm.

While being incapacitated, I had a chance to reflect on my life, my career and my present circumstances. Living in LA had been a real struggle. Financially, I had been hanging on by a thread with no sign of getting rich any time soon. I had no one to call on. The few that I knew who had money let me know up front their money was handled by an attorney. In other words, don't ask.

At Christmas, I never received a Christmas card except from the Funks. The tunes I had been a part of bore no significance to anyone. It was like I was an alien from another planet.

I remained in the hospital for a few days and convalesced at home. I followed the doctor's orders precisely, and recovered even quicker than expected.

After being released by the doctor, it was time to seek work again. I didn't want to go to Motown and ask for favors or anything else, but I had to at least try to do something to help my situation.

I knew Barney Ales was at Motown and I was once the vice president of his company in Detroit. He shut his company down to go to LA which seemed to have been a re-enactment of how Motown deserted Detroit. No warning, no word, no nothing. It was like they were reading lines from the same script. Thelma Laverette had to shut the company down.

Maybe since he knows me, I thought, he might 'throw me a bone'. I pondered about whether or not to go, and finally decided that I had nothing to lose. I went to Motown, but I wasn't allowed to see Barney. I wasn't surprised. It was back to square one.

There is an old cliché that says if it seems too good to be true, then it probably is. I learned this lesson the hard way and paid dearly.

I was approached by an acquaintance who seemed very 'legit' and he had a deal for me that I couldn't refuse. All of the paperwork, license plates and everything about the entire deal seemed perfect. I'm speaking of a car I bought from a guy, drove it for a year and was surprised when I was arrested for receiving a stolen car.

This just couldn't be happening to me, I thought, but it was. The truth hit me like a Mack Truck driven at 100 mph. I was already two miles past nowhere with my life and now this.

My first thought was, how can I ever explain this without sounding like a complete fool? It wasn't possible. At my hearing the judge could readily understand that I was a victim and not a criminal. I was definitely out of my element. If my record hadn't been squeaky clean, I might have had to wear a striped suit. I bought a car at a good price, but in the end I paid a bigger price. For me, that was one of life's greatest lessons. What a lesson!

The 'noose' of life had tightened a little bit more around my neck and I was about to choke. I had to make a vital decision about moving or staying in California, and I had to be quick about it. I discussed my options with Char, which were to stay in LA and perish or move back east. After carefully thinking through our problem we decided to move to Tennessee.

This is where Char's family lived. Memphis, Tennessee was our choice.

It was OK, but Memphis didn't even have a Musicians' Union. Musically, the possibilities were few and none. I wondered how this saga would work out. I had to try it no matter what. I figured I was so low I could only go one way now, and that was up.

I drove down to see Eddie Bongo and to inform him of our decision to move. He didn't look like the old Eddie and expressed how tired he was of begging for work. It was hard to talk about music and not speak of the shortcomings at Motown.

"You know that we should not have been in this predicament. We made too many people rich to be broke ourselves," Eddie cried.

I agreed and went on to say, "I had a feeling that this day would someday come. That's the reason why I tried to get something going in

Detroit years ago."

Eddie sadly dropped his head and his voice trembled as he said, "It's a damn shame no provisions were made for us. I don't know what I'm gonna do, and there's no help in sight. My wife keeps the rent paid, but you know I like to take care of my own. I don't want my wife taking care of me."

I had to cut my conversation short, and told Eddie the day I planned to move. He told me he would come out and give me a hand. He did just that and stayed until the truck was completely loaded.

"Well, Bo-Wankles" (Eddie called me that name sometimes), "Don't forget about me. Call me sometimes because I may not be able to call you."

With assurance I said, "You know I'll keep in touch, and as soon as I get a chance, I'll be back." We embraced, clinging to each other for several moments. Neither of us could say anything else. We just stood and stared at each other. I realized Eddie didn't look too well, but I had no idea this would be the last time I would ever see him alive. In less than a year, he was dead.

A memorial was held for him in LA with funeral services and burial in Detroit. With the news of him passing, I became very grieved. It was doubly painful because it hadn't been very long since Jamerson passed away. I wallowed in my own sorrow because I didn't have plane fare to attend Eddie's final service. I can't begin to tell you how much that hurt me.

I made the trip to Tennessee alone with the furniture. My wife and children were already there. We didn't have a place of our own to live in. My wife's sister Helen and brother-in-law Willie Joe had a family of their own, but extended every courtesy to us.

We stayed in a converted garage, and we slept on a hide-a-bed sofa.

We worked for two months, saved our money, and then got our own apartment. Without their help I can't imagine what we would have done. It was the helping hand that we needed and I will always love and appreciate them for being so kind to us..

I wanted the memories of my shortcomings to just fade away, but frame by frame, my past became a slide show that never ceased to exhibit vivid images of yesterday. I felt myself sinking into a pit of nothingness, but it was too difficult to alter the paths of fate.

My resilience and courage had taken a back seat and I had fallen from grace and found refuge in my bedroom for several months. The outside

Chips, Me and Hattie Little on the road with Marvin Gaye

Vibes and drums in the 'Snake Pit'.

George McGregor (drummer) – 1970

Bobby Martin (producer) 1978

Jimmy Pavlack and Eddie Parker at
Ashford Records in 1974

Ray Monette from Rare Earth

With Joe Zawinul at the 2003 Grammys

Me and (inset) Char with Milt Jackson in 1979

Back on stage with the vibes and the Funk Brothers in 2003

With Bootsie Collins and the 'Bar-Mitzvah guitarist' who changed our lives, Allen 'Dr Licks' Slutsky, in 2000

With Pistol and Uriel in 1998

With Johnny Griffith, 2000

With Bob Babbitt, 2000

Uriel Jones and Richard 'Pistol' Allen, 1998

With Ben Harper, 2000.

With Bob Babbitt, backing Chaka Khan, 2003

With Joan Osborne., 2003

L to R: Johnny Griffith, Montel Jordan, Jay Butler and me, 2000

In the Motown Museum.

The Funks play Austin, Texas in 2003

On the beach in 1999

My sister-in-law and brother, Helen and Joe Harris

Grandson, Evan, in the Snake Pit, looking at Jack's vibes, 2000

A family moment in Detroit in the year 2000. From left to right: oldest daughter, Miko, Jack, Ch youngest daughter, Jakene.

world was my enemy. That undaunted tenacity that was once present had weakened and I became enfeebled from life's upper cuts and right crosses. At times I staggered, but I was never knocked out. I refused to fall.

I awoke one day and realized that I couldn't spend the rest of my life inside. It was time for me to 'grab life by the horns' and make a complete transformation. The realization was clear, but I was still licking my wounds. I began to read the classified ads and naturally the word music was nowhere in the entire paper. The ads had little to offer except for jobs like fork lifters, truck drivers, waiters, welders, and security work.

I was once a welder but twenty-five years had passed, and those skills were non existent. As much as I didn't want security work, it was about the only job I could do.

A friend in Detroit who was really trying to help advanced me a package that promised to sell and make millions. She said this product was selling in Detroit and making astronomical amounts of money. I agreed to try a case. In a few days I had my very own starter kit of 'Roach Buster', a powder to exterminate roaches. I became known as the "Roach Powder Man." I sold the first kit in no time at all because everybody in the complex had roaches. My profit was a whopping sixty dollars.

The second case was more difficult to sell because I had to seek new clients away from my apartment. In short it didn't work.

I didn't really enjoy company at home but this particular night was different. My wife's cousin, Geraldine Smith Tolbert, joined us for dinner. She was a very sincere and spiritually inspired young lady. She spoke of how God had blessed her and she encouraged me to continue to pray. As we conversed, I mentioned that I didn't have a job and needed one badly. She told me about a security job opening where she worked. She gave me the phone number and the person's name to see. I followed through and after the interview I had the job.

I thanked God for leading Geraldine to our dinner table that night, and consider her a key person in helping me to give my life a 'jump start'. I will always love her and reserve a special place in my heart for her. On that job, I worked my way up to security manager and made it pay off for me until the store closed. I didn't allow grass to grow beneath my feet, I was off to another job – a security job.

On my new security job, I secured the property of several stores by monitoring the outside in a vehicle. Some days I would drive over a hundred miles around the parking lot. I often thought about the fact that this was far from music, and found it hard to believe that I was so far out of the loop. Some days I would take my tapes and write lyrics, but on other days I had plenty of time to take Geraldine's advice and pray for something better.

One day another miracle happened and I met a Mrs. Robinson. We talked about music and she told me about her involvement as a personal manager. It sounded a little strange, and I wondered why would an artist need a manager in this town. I figured I would tell my strange story which was that I recorded on many of the Motown releases. I waited for her to tell me that I was crazy, but instead she believed me and became very interested and excited.

Her questions were comparable to a magazine interviewer. She told me about a local businessman who wanted to launch his own record company and who could use my expertise. She felt we needed to talk. (Did we ever need to talk?) She told me about a Halloween party where one of her artists would be performing and this business man, Terry Starks, would also be attending.

My wife and I went to the party. (By the way, I went as my favorite character, Dracula.) Mrs. Robinson introduced me to Terry, we talked and after about three additional meetings, Terry hired me as the assistant to the president of Mega Jam Records.

This was the closest I had been to happiness in years. At last I was back into the record business. This didn't seem remotely possible just a short time ago, but now I was in charge of operations for a new and upcoming company in Memphis Tennessee. I felt rejuvenated and alive again. It took a couple of months to put the company together and establish each department. Everything was going well until the owner fell victim to outside influences that lowered my comfort level. I could see the company winding downward before the first record was released. My efforts and leadership were eventually rejected.

I began networking with another record company 'wannabe', who misrepresented himself and convinced me to join his company. That was another mistake.

Thank goodness those episodes were short lived. Shortly after I left, both companies closed. The idea of a record company was great, but these men were not in any way ready for such a thing.

After the close of the record companies, it was back to ground zero.

My wife had to be off from work on sick leave from her job and our accumulated savings were diminishing rapidly. I had been hit and wounded by a series of adversities, but I had to somehow slay these demons and move on with the rest of my life. I reviewed the classified ads again. Naturally there wasn't anything related to the record business. I had a few skills in selling and decided to try being a coffee salesman. I became one of the best they ever had. My mom had taught me the principles by which she lived and that was do your best no matter what the task. I wasn't doing what I wanted to be doing but I was making a living. It was somewhat demeaning, but I was getting paid.

Knock! Knock! It was opportunity knocking again. My friend Elmo told me about one of his acquaintances that needed an assistant in his construction company. That was just great since I had a zero aptitude in the area of construction business.

I boldly contacted Gary Crum and made an appointment with him. He was impressed with how articulate I was and said he would train me in the necessary areas. I almost fell to my knees when he said, "You're hired." This had to be another one of those unexplained miracles because I certainly didn't possess the necessary qualifications. I worked with Gary for a couple of years and then established my own construction company.

I did well with satisfying insurance claims until the construction 'sharks' wanted my business. Instead of competing, they tried to sink me and my reputation in order to have all of the business. Eventually they were successful and I had to close my company.

I couldn't understand the personal attacks and frankly until today I still fail to understand.

Life's circumstances had me on the ropes but I wasn't about to be knocked out. My construction business had closed, I didn't have a job, and I felt like I was praying from the pits of hell. My inner faith confirmed that the mysteries of life weren't really mysteries, but God's perfect timing of the lows and highs that will be disseminated as he sees fit.

I sometimes wondered if I had brought a karma from another life into this one. Had I been sentenced to thirty years of suffering? What was my destiny? The drive, the stamina and the ability to continue fighting were all of the things that led to my downfall in Memphis, Tennessee.

People in this town rejected and opposed those qualities from me. Being aggressive and displaying the ability to do straight up business was not appreciated and Memphians held me with mistrust. Aggressiveness just wasn't appreciated. I can truly say that I came in contact with all of the dregs of Memphis society in trying to succeed. Since I was not a native of Memphis I believe that was a strike against me, and I was very misunderstood. All of the unfortunate conditions were temporary setbacks, not a final defeat.

I remember a conversation I had with a friend, Janie Bradford. She explained, "If you submit your entire resumé on an application people won't believe your qualifications and will reject you for being out of your realm of capabilities. You'll appear to be too big and they'll wonder why you are applying. People will think you're overqualified or they will think you're lying."

Janie was correct. I remember on job interviews I seemed to get the attention of the examiner for a few minutes as I revealed some of the things that I had accomplished. This all usually led to, "Well, we don't have any positions open at this time", or "We'll call you if something comes up."

As unpleasant as I found Memphis, I managed to wade through the sea of unkind and cruel circumstances to find another job to help to maintain the family. It was back to the security business. Security jobs were easy to find and in no time I had landed another job. I really worked hard to do a good job and was recognized for doing well. It took a lot out of me because sometimes I found myself in dangerous situations face to face with a variety of criminals who resisted any kind of opposition.

In 1990 the telephone rang one day when I was on my way to work. Speaking from the other end was a guy named Allen Slutsky who had the strangest message. "I wrote a book about James Jamerson and I would like to make a movie about the Funk Brothers."

These words were numbing. This was unbelievable! I have been kicked in the butt for a couple of decades and now this guy wants to do something nice for me and the Funks? I wondered what he was smoking or was it a cruel joke. "You want to do a movie on the Funk Brothers?" I questioned.

We talked on and he assured me that he was sincere and would be calling again to get more information. I hung the phone up without getting this guy's phone number or any information about him.

"Char, there was a guy on the phone that said he wants to do a movie on the Funk Brothers" She asked me to repeat what I said, and we both laughed.

She sarcastically reminded me, "Don't quit your day job!"

This Slutsky guy really got my attention and I looked forward to his next call. It took longer than I wanted before I heard from him again. In about a month the calls came in regularly as he started putting the script together. I found Allen Slutsky quite loquacious, and he probably thought the same of me because I had a lot to impart about my life as a Funk Brother. Whenever he interviewed me I could anticipate at least an hour of questions and answers. I loved reliving those days at Motown, and besides it gave me an opportunity to withdraw from the appalling experiences I encountered in Memphis.

MORE PRODUCERS

Berry Gordy

Berry Gordy has invariably been perceived as the founder and owner of the most extraordinary record enterprise in the world… Motown Records. That just goes without even saying. However, most people have never recognized him as a competent record producer. It has always just been Berry Gordy, CEO, overlooking those talents that likely enhanced his chances of becoming successful.

He was a very good songwriter who understood the important components of a song and taught those skills to those who worked for him. Producing was done by his standards as well.

These skills as a songwriter and producer also likely enabled him to recognize those that didn't quite have what it took to be in the Motown arena. I don't think anyone is foolish enough to think that the company's success was by accident and everything was on 'automatic pilot'.

Berry's music aptitude was an intrinsic factor that led to putting Motown on top. He was quite perceptive and his A&R skills allowed him to masterfully select the right artist with each song. It has been said that his storytelling ability went right along with his development as a songwriter.

Probably one of his first songs that he co-wrote that people remember is 'Reet Petite', recorded by Jackie Wilson. After that, Berry recorded co-written songs with his sister Gwen and her husband Billy. They recorded 'To Be Loved', 'We Have Love', 'That's Why (I Love Her So).'

I think that this was just setting the stage for others who would flock to that famous address on West Grand Boulevard. His gut feelings and his almost impeccable ability to 'hear' hits helped to manifest what may have seemed like a dimly imagined possibility to some.

Let me say here that in spite of Berry's abilities to critique and pick songs he almost missed on one of Motown's biggest releases, 'What's Going On?' by Marvin Gaye. He *didn't* 'hear it' at first and had almost decided to 'can it'. Boy! That would have been a big blunder.

I often wondered did Berry have a particular formula to evaluate a song. I learned that it was just simplicity and the uniqueness of words. Two verses, a bridge, a chorus and then back to the verse, one more chorus and then the fade. That seemed to have been the general method of composing hits. At first, I thought maybe he was a celebrated musician. He wasn't great on the piano, but he could play well enough to do what he needed.

Another one of Berry's early productions was 'Come To Me' by Marv Johnson.

'Money (That's What I Want)' and 'Shop Around' were two projects that Berry had a sizeable part in the production of. So in retrospect, Berry cannot be overlooked as a producer. He really did it all.

Nick Ashford and Valerie Simpson

Nick and Valerie were just beautiful people to work with. They came to Motown with the help of Holland-Dozier-Holland. These two hailed from New York and seemed a little different in their fashion and their quiet demeanor. With just the sight of their arrival the whispers started and minds began to wonder just what these two were about.

Without any doubt or question, they were about the business of writing and producing hit records. They were competitive. They are best known for their productions of 'Ain't Nothing Like The Real Thing', 'You're All I Need To Get By', 'Reach Out And Touch' and 'Solid As A Rock'. They wrote very positive songs that depicted their personalities.

This dynamic couple was very respected around the company and known as the 'Motown Sweethearts'. Their relationship developed into a long-lasting marriage and they are still married today. Their tenure at Motown ended around the same time in 1973 when Motown closed its doors. They always maintained their residence in New York so it was just a matter of returning home.

Nick's family and my family hail from North Carolina. Everybody always asks if we are related. There's a likely chance that we are cousins. We have never dug deeply into our family roots, but there are many coincidental circumstances that seem to match. Our physical statures are similar. We're both tall, slender, about the same color and we look a little alike. We have promised each other that one day we'll verify our suspicion.

Our meeting again since 1973 was very heartwarming and very touching. We were united in New York at the Apollo for the *Standing In The Shadows of Motown* screening, and show. They were as charming as ever and their performance on the show was superb. They exemplify love at its best.

Weldon A. McDougal III

Weldon was often referred to as the 'Motown Promotion Guru'. He had his introduction to the music industry well before his entrance to Motown. He was a part of a group known as the Larks and he also formed Hawthorne Productions whose roster embraced Eddie Holman, The Volcanoes, Barbara Mason, and several others.

Weldon was a proud and uncompromising person who always caught everyone's attention by announcing his full name, 'Weldon A. McDougall III'. The brilliance and professionalism of his work goes unchallenged, with a legendary list of artists and records he systematically promoted, and he was responsible for their tunes leaving the DJs' turntables and reaching the airways across the country.

It would be difficult to talk about Motown and not mention Weldon's name because of the important role he played in making the stars successful.

"I first met Jack when I started my label with Johnny Styles and Luther Randolph at Hawthorne Records and we used Jack to play on several tunes," Weldon explained.

After one of the sessions, Weldon and I were talking and I was telling him about the offer Marvin Gaye had made Charles Harris and me to go to Detroit soon.

He wished me well and thought that was an excellent opportunity. Charles and I went to Detroit as planned.

The next time that I saw Weldon was at Motown. "Man, what are you doing here?" I asked.

"I'm a promotion man, Berry hired me."

We talked about Philly and walked on down to the Snake Pit. "I actually came by to bum a joint from one of the musicians," Weldon said.

"Well, I don't smoke, but sometime when you're in town stop by and meet Char and see my new baby Miko," I said.

He never gave up his home in Philadelphia, and whenever I was there I would call or go by. At the close of Motown, he went to work for Gamble and Huff at Philly International. He remained there for seven years. Many years have passed but we have always maintained our friendship.

"I met this guy around 1993 by the name of Allen Slutsky (Dr. Licks) who had written a book about James Jamerson and said that he wanted to talk to some musicians who had worked as studio musicians with James Jamerson. I immediately thought of Jack and gave Allen his telephone number.

"Sure enough Allen called Jack and explained his plan, which was unbelievable but was well received. Jack called and thanked me for the hook up.

"Several years passed and we would talk from time to time but on this one particular call Jack said that the Funk Brothers would be traveling to Detroit to be in a documentary about them and the next thing I know, I see the movie *Standing In The Shadows of Motown*.

"Thank God! It couldn't have happened to a nicer group of guys," Weldon declared.

I wish that I had half the pictures that Weldon has. He snapped photographs of somebody everyday when he was at Motown. He says, "I have stacks of pictures that I've never shown to anybody."

I asked him "What sparked your interest in photography?"

He said, "I went to the barber shop one day and the guys were bad rapping Marvin Gaye and I told them what they were saying wasn't true. Of course, they wanted to know how I knew anything about Marvin. I told them that I was with him all of the time promoting his records. In disbelief they told me to get out of the barber shop because they didn't think that I was telling the truth. To prove them wrong, I went out and bought a Polaroid camera.

"When Marvin did the 'High Lit Show' on channel 48, I took pictures. When I went back to the barbershop I had pictures to prove that I worked with Marvin.

"That was just the beginning. When I worked with The Jackson 5, they all had expensive cameras. One time when they were singing the National anthem at the baseball World Series I took their pictures. Michael showed me all of the functions of the camera and I thought that was quite interesting, and to top things off, a man offered me cash money for the film I had taken of the Jackson 5. He said that he was a reporter. I got permission from Tito and we sold the film and split the hundred dollars 50/50. The money aspect was very interesting.

"I ended up buying my own camera. On the other hand just standing around was a pain in the neck and taking pictures gave me something to do while working. In spite of places where pictures were prohibited, I still got shots of artists because of my affiliation with Motown. So I have pictures that no one else in the world has."

Since Weldon promoted so many artists, I wondered did he have a favorite.

He told me, "When I would go out with any act, I would see them night after night. After watching the show that first night, it would be hard to sit and watch the show again and again. I have been out with Marvin Gaye, Stevie Wonder, Bobby Taylor, Gladys Knight and the Pips, The Temptations, Shorty Long and even Sammy Davis Jr.

"Now with Sammy Davis Jr. I would never miss a performance because he was so entertaining. Every time he went on stage I was right there. He was so versatile. I guess that I didn't really consider him a true Motown artist, because he was a superstar long before he came to Motown.

"I liked every Motown act because they were all so nice to me. I promoted them equally and cared about them equally. One night on a promotion tour in Philly with Marvin Gaye when we went back to the hotel, there were several young ladies waiting. One said, 'We would like to go to your room and sit and talk to you.'

"So Marvin was very nice about it and invited them up. He was a gentleman about the whole thing. When we got to the room Marvin ordered food and drinks for everybody. One of the young ladies surprised us with her invitation to Marvin. 'I have always wanted to make love to you, would you mind?' The other young ladies said, 'We don't mind, go on.'

"Marvin just smiled and said, 'I'm sorry but I don't do nothing like that.'

"I shook my head in disappointment thinking that with three girls I could have been able to get at least one. I had never had that opportunity that Marvin had because I wasn't a star."

When the movie was premiered in Philadelphia, Weldon went to see it. He called with excitement in his voice. "The movie is great! The reaction from the audience is like nothing I've ever seen in my life. People stood up and cheered and clapped after the performance! I can't believe what I saw! I want to make a prediction that *Standing in the Shadows of Motown* is gonna win an Oscar. I just feel happy for all of the good things that's finally happening to the Funk Brothers."

Ernest Kelly

Ernest Kelly arrived at Motown from New York and was Hank Cosby's assistant. Kelly was very smooth talking and quite thorough on the job. His business ethics were laced with cleverness and frankness. That fast moving New York portion of his character could be easily observed with his attorney-like approach to business. This guy's wardrobe wasn't bad either.

Like me, Ernest saw an opportunity to launch his independent company and joined forces first with Johnny Griffith. Of course, Johnny was a Dunn & Bradstreet wannabe.

Kelly was exactly what he needed to keep both of his feet on the ground. Their business spiraled downward, and Kelly then became a well known promotion man. During the late sixties, Kelly joined my team as co-owner of Triple B Records with Lorraine and me. His promotional contacts and effort were an asset to the company. We were not bound by any long term contracts or agreements so when the company 'fizzed out' we just went our separate ways.

Hal Davis

Hal Davis was considered to be a west coast producer whose home was in Cincinnati, Ohio. We called him 'Mr. Motown', which was so befitting due to the untiring hours he spent grinding in the studio. We're talking about twelve, fourteen or sixteen hours a day plus.

He also managed the west coast operations for a while.

There's a couple of things in particular that I remember about Hal. First, he was a real gentleman with a lot of compassion. He treated everybody with respect and was well liked. Secondly, it seemed that he never needed me on a session until late at night. On his sessions, I usually arrived at the studio around 2:00 a.m. In spite of the hour, the place would usually be packed with people. I would almost have to squeeze my way in to the control room. Sometimes he would have Susie Ikeda and Clifton Davis there. He would have liquor and food as though it was a big party. He seemed to observe everyone's reaction to each tune. I had a song I wrote that I wanted him to record. I played it for him and he said, "This is a great tune and I know just who this would be a good song for – Jermaine Jackson."

The name of the song was 'Things Just Won't Be The Same'. This was good news for me since we were going to co-produce the tune. We put down a very rocking track with strings and all we needed was to complete the vocals and take it to Berry.

Jermaine tried but just couldn't handle the song. I laid down the demo track and when Berry heard it, he said "Jack should be singing this song." We went back and forth about who would sing the song and eventually lost the project.

Hal produced hits on The Jackson 5, 'Got To Be There', Diana Ross, 'Love Hangover', Thelma Houston, 'Don't Leave Me This Way', Brenda Holloway, 'Every Little Bit Hurts', and he also cut some tunes on Junior Walker. Hal had several hits, but they were all produced on the West coast.

I remember Hal called me once after a recording session with Thelma Houston's 'Don't Leave Me This Way.' As usual it was about the same time he called me for the other overdubs and sessions. It was about 4:00 am. This was in 1976, at Paramount Studios on Santa Monica. It turned out to be a monumental date. He explained he had cut this great song, knew it was a smash, but it was lacking something. He said, "This song needs your tambourine to drive it on home."

After listening to the play-back and comparing the difference, he was definitely correct. If you listen halfway through the song you'll hear the tambourine pick it up and take it on to the world of gold and platinum. The rhythm on this session was done by west coast musicians.

There is one funny story about Hal that I still sometimes chuckle about. There was a celebration at a Hollywood club in conjunction with the debut release of a record.

They served wine and cheese along with expensive gourmet dishes. It was probably a J-5 release because there were so many radio personalities, musicians, recording artists, and anybody that was anybody, along with a long list of Hal's friends.

Hal arrived in a big long limo. As soon as he got inside, this startling drop-dead Halle Berry type beautiful, shapely, voluptuous woman immediately was all over him. She was all over him like a cheap suit. Hal just smiled and enjoyed every moment. He had a special way of sharing a drink with a lady by putting his arm in her arm and sort of 'locking' the two together.

As he began sharing his drink with the lady, some of the guys started laughing. I couldn't imagine what was so funny because from what I could see he had the finest woman in the place. They began kissing rather passionately. U-m-m I thought to myself, it won't be long before they'll be leaving going home. Well sure enough they started heading for the door just as I thought. The limo pulled up and Hal and his lady sped off. They were all over each other and I was still wondering why the guys were laughing. As Hal and the lady pulled off someone yelled, "That's a dude that left with Hal, that ain't no woman."

We howled with laughter. Later on in the week, I was in Hal's office and I asked "What happened when you left the club the other night with that woman?"

He looked at me as though he wanted to kill me and said, "Man I don't ever want to even talk about that again. I can't begin to tell you how disappointed I was. I wish I'd written that song, you can't judge a book by its cover." I thought that we would never finish laughing.

He passed away without me knowing until a year later.

Clay McMurray

Clay McMurray was another Motown producer brought in by Norman Whitfield. He was best known for his production of 'If I Were Your Woman and You Were My Man'.

This tune was cut on Gladys Knight. I consider him to be a very talented guy and very nice to work with. During his tenure at Motown, he had a very close relationship with Norman Whitfield and they were 'running partners'. They combed the night clubs almost every night for new talent and concepts.

On any given night you could find them at the Twenty Grand night club. They would be observing how people reacted to certain songs and which songs were popular. This kind of activity seemed to stimulate their own skills and helped them to create that next hit. When Clay and Norman dissolved their relationship, Norman wrote a song called 'Plastic Man'. Norman said that it was written to describe Clay.

Like many others, Clay ventured west to LA seeking a continuation of what he had experienced in Detroit. Logically it seemed right, but it just wasn't the case. 'The great brick wall' that we all encountered was still standing there waiting for another victim – Clay McMurray.

After a few years of unfavorable gains he returned to Detroit.

THE MAKING OF THE DOCUMENTARY

After numerous interviews with Allen Slutsky for about ten years, in preparation of gathering information for the documentary, the phone finally rang one gloomy rainy day with Allen on the other end. He was quite excited and he sounded as though he was hyperventilating, trying to explain he had secured funding and he had dates, times and places reserved for the Funks.

He said that we would be starting on the documentary the first week in December, 2000. After hearing all he had to say and absorbing it, I was hyperventilating too!

There had been so many years of planning and promises, I wasn't totally convinced. I still had my doubts. I knew that Allen was sincere, but in spite of that it was still a little unbelievable. I was like 'Doubting Thomas' in the Bible.

The Funks had been so down for so long, I was still agnostic until I received my itinerary and a confirmation that Eddie Willis and I had a van reserved to travel into Detroit.

This was still unimaginable. We – the Funk Brothers would be involved in making our very own documentary. Somebody pinch me to see if I'm dreaming! For years, I had been like a fish floundering in a near dried stream, but now at last I could visualize a torrential rain filling the river and the swift currents sweeping me away to the deep waters.

This was just the first true realization that Allen's tenacity and 'bulldog' courage would finally manifest as he had promised. THANK YOU GOD!!! Thank you so much! And thanks to that little 48-year-old, self-described 'bar mitzvah musician' from New Jersey named Allen Slutsky!

Eddie Willis and I made final arrangements to meet and set a time to leave for the Motor City. Without losing any time, Eddie drove to my house in Memphis from Mississippi. After kissing our wives and hugging the dog, we were on our way.

The level of excitement was still immense. After all, this was comparable to the Super Bowl, only this time it was about *us*. We were the players in a game with the winning score already determined for my team. It felt so good-d-d-d!

Eddie and I drove passionately with one objective in mind – get to

Detroit quick, fast, and in a hurry. We talked and reminisced about our days in the Funk Factory and how we became outsiders looking in.

How we wished all of the Funks were living and could be a part of this. As always the highway had its way of tranquilizing me. I was all the way in dream land when I was so rudely awakened by squelching tires and a big thump. I quickly raised up and all I could see was Bambi's four hoofs and it being knocked into an eighteen wheeler. Eddie had hit a deer. The left fender was damaged, but not enough to stop us.

I eventually repaired the fender with crazy glue and duct tape. In what seemed to be a short time, we were less than four hundred miles to Detroit. I couldn't sleep any more after that. We stopped for gas and I took the wheel and continued on and drove the remaining miles.

We were the last to arrive. Our apartment was waiting for us on 13 Mile Road. Allen had arranged for us to live at a completely furnished corporate apartment. Johnny Griffith and Bob Babbitt shared another apartment. Allen stayed with his friend Craig Weeland in his house in the sleepy little suburb of Detroit, Lavonia, Michigan,

After settling in, we were given directions to Craig's house. Everybody was there. Allen's assistant Paul Justman, Craig, Joe Hunter, Joe Messina, Uriel Jones, Bob Babbitt, Johnny Griffith, Pistol Allen, and of course Eddie and me. (At that time neither Pistol nor Johnny appeared to be ill, but they are both deceased now.)

This tribe of brothers met again with emotions running rampant, and tears of joy trickling from our faces as we embraced and all stood in the same room for the first time in thirty years.

We were ecstatic. Nature's paint brush had colored our hair gray and tracks of time had now begun to show, with wrinkles and pronounced laugh lines. What used to be six packs was now a bunch of round bellies. Our ages now ranged from 61 to 73. Practically everybody wore glasses now. We had pill boxes of medicines to take for various health problems and we joked about our different ailments.

We were without any question out of shape physically, but nothing, absolutely nothing, had changed our affection and long standing love for each other.

This fraternity of Funk Brothers stood torn and tattered from the rough high seas of life, but our spirits gleamed and merged like diamonds in the rough. There were no superficial smiles, just whoops of laughter and joy.

I'm sure that there were those that looked upon us as inane creatures or the 'has-beens' of the industry, but we would now have the opportunity to have those erroneous assumptions put to rest. It was like the world had stopped spinning to allow us to get on again. Our exuberance was bubbling over and the feeling that I had is beyond words of description. The rapid heartbeats of pleasure simply overwhelmed me.

Craig's basement area was used for practicing daily until the crew was ready for shooting the film. We welcomed this opportunity to practice and get our 'chops up' again.

After the sheet music was passed out, and the first round of practice, it was evident we still 'had it'. We were as good as any day in the sixties when we cut sessions all day and night seven days a week. "We still have it! We still have it!" I shouted.

Allen probably felt some anxiety about how we would recreate those same licks, but he never disclosed or divulged his concerns.

Actually, I think we surprised ourselves with the rhythm being so tight and we sounded basically the same. In a couple of days we began rehearsing with the background singers, Carla Benson, Keith Benson, Cherokee Pree, Johnny Ingram, Delbert Nelson, Misty Love, Dawn Blandford, Kizzy Jester, and the IDMR Detroit Choir. Rudy Robinson along with a reporter Ben Edmonds from Mojo magazine, Engineer Steve Smith, and Susan Whithall were all there. There were plenty of refreshments and food at every session.

The weather became quite inclement with snow falling practically every day. Getting to and from practice grew more difficult daily with the constant accumulation of snow. The ride from Royal Oak to Lavonia was normally less than forty minutes, but with the snow, our drive time doubled and tripled. In spite of the weather conditions we found a lot of warmth and sunshine even in the snow.

After so many days of practicing, we were ready to record the sound track for the documentary.

The musicians who had remained nameless, and had played on so many hit songs, would now make their first move from the background to the front stage. It took some thirty years to get here, but I can't question God's perfect timing. The stage was set and cameras were ready to roll at the Royal Oak Music Theatre. It was an unknown place to us, but it felt like we were playing at the 'Garden' in New York City.

My heart cried for the Funk Brothers who had fallen before this day. Oh how I wish they could be a part of this.

Allen started researching his biography of James Jamerson in 1986, which promoted his interest to research the other Funk Brothers and led to the creation of the film.

"I can't believe we're really here," Allen explained to a reporter. "But I won't exhale until the film's in the can and we have a backup tape. Then, when it's over, the world will know what these guys did.

The film was directed by Paul Justman, and taped during the month of December 2000 at several locations. In order to recreate the total sound, several artists were brought in to record on the tracks. '(Love Is Like A) Heat Wave' and 'What Becomes Of The Broken Hearted – Joan Osborne, 'You Really Got A Hold On Me' and 'Cloud Nine' – Me'Shell NdegéOcello, 'Do You Love Me?' and 'Cool Jerk' – Bootsy Collins, 'Reach Out I'll Be There' and 'Shotgun' – Gerald Levert, 'Ain't Too Proud To Beg' and 'I Heard It Through The Grapevine' – Ben Harper, 'What's Going On?' – Chaka Khan and 'Ain't No Mountain High Enough' – Chaka Khan and Montel Williams. The soundtrack has been nominated for a Grammy, featuring Chaka Khan on 'What's Going On?'*

All of the recognition is great, grand and wonderful but we can't overlook the fact that Berry granted us permission to use thirty Motown songs in the documentary.

"Berry did a cool thing," Allen said. "Nobody gets to use thirty Motown songs in a movie."

I am very grateful and so are all of the other Funks.

POEMS

Whispers

They spoke of us in whispered tones,
And about how well we played,
We smiled and kept on making hits,
We thought we had it made.

Broken Hearts

There is no cure for broken hearts,
They are beyond repair,
But in the dust of passing time,
There are still some feeling there.
Some of us have left this world,
Sad and broken hearted.
It was hard for us to understand,
How things changed from the way we started.

A look At The Funks

The Funk Brothers were a special group,
That came from different places,
We had a mixture of many talents,
And some from different races,
But all for one and one for all,
Our talents stood the test,
We charted almost all we cut,
We stood tall above the rest.

Index

Acknowledgements

The publishers would like to thank Martha Reeves, Paul Elliot of ES Films, Graham Finch, and anyone else who has contributed to this book. Your help is very much appreciated. We are also grateful for the kind assistance given to the project by Billy Williams of the Motown Alumni Association and David Meikle and Lowell Boileau of SoulfulDetroit. Every effort has been made to acknowledge contributions and we apologise for any oversights, which we will be happy to address in future editions.

Printed in the United Kingdom
by Lightning Source UK Ltd.
129511UK00002B/96/A

The Collected
Supernatural and Weird Fiction of Bram Stoker Volume 5